Sustainability and Agile Project Management

Sustainable project management is a new school of management thought and a growing trend, yet there is a scarcity of research on the linkage between individual project management methodologies and sustainability in projects. This book fills a gap through theoretical and empirical research on the implications of sustainability in project management and, in particular, agile project management.

The book explores three main themes. First, it identifies and assesses the validity of the application of the concepts of sustainable development in the family of agile methodological frameworks. Second, the research results are presented as an introduction to further in-depth research on the future relationships between sustainable development and agile project management. Third, the book identifies the competencies that are needed to successfully implement projects in the context of sustainable development.

Sustainability and Agile Project Management will be of direct appeal to academics and scholars in the field of management sciences, including project management, corporate governance and human resource management.

Katarzyna Piwowar-Sulej, PhD, DSc, is Associate Professor at the Wroclaw University of Economics and Business, Poland. She is also Head of Postgraduate Studies for Business Trainers and Postgraduate Studies for 'Management 3.0'. Her research interests include sustainable human resource management, sustainable project management. She has experience in managing HR departments, leading HR and HR-IT projects in business, and leading and participating in various research projects.

Mariusz Sołtysik, PhD, is Assistant Professor in the Management Process Department at Cracow University of Economics,, Poland. Her research interests include strategic management, project management and innovations. Her articles are published in *Science of the Total Environment*, *Environmental Impact Assessment Review*, *Business Strategy and the Environment*, *Sustainable Development* and the *Journal of Organizational Change Management*.

Routledge Frontiers in Project Management

Edited by Darren Dalcher

Project management has become a key competence for most organisations in the public and private sectors. Driven by recent business trends such as fewer management layers, greater flexibility, increasing geographical distribution and more project-based work, project management has grown beyond its roots in the construction, engineering and aerospace industries to transform the service, financial, computer, and general management sectors. In fact, a *Fortune* article rated project management as the number one career choice at the beginning of the 21st century. Yet many organisations have struggled in applying the traditional models of project management to their new projects in the global environment.

Project management offers a framework to help organisations to transform their mainstream operations and service performance. It is viewed as a way of organising for the future. Moreover, in an increasingly busy, stressful, and uncertain world it has become necessary to manage several projects successfully at the same time. According to some estimates the world annually spends well over $10 trillion (US) on projects. In the UK alone, more than £250 billion is spent on projects every year. Up to half of these projects fail! A major ingredient in the build-up leading to failure is often cited as the lack of adequate project management knowledge and experience. Some organisations have responded to this situation by trying to improve the understanding and capability of their managers and employees who are introduced to projects, as well as their experienced project managers in an attempt to enhance their competence and capability in this area.

Routledge Frontiers in Project Management provides short, state of play, guides to the main aspects of the new emerging applications including: maturity models, agile projects, extreme projects, six sigma and projects, human factors and leadership in projects, project governance, value management, virtual teams, project benefits.

Sustainability and Agile Project Management
Methodologies for Sustainable Development
Edited by Katarzyna Piwowar-Sulej and Mariusz Sołtysik

For more information about this series, please visit: www.routledge.com/Routledge-Frontiers-in-Project-Management/book-series/RFPM

Sustainability and Agile Project Management

Methodologies for Sustainable Development

Edited by Katarzyna Piwowar-Sulej and Mariusz Sołtysik

Routledge
Taylor & Francis Group
LONDON AND NEW YORK

First published 2025
by Routledge
4 Park Square, Milton Park, Abingdon, Oxon OX14 4RN

and by Routledge
605 Third Avenue, New York, NY 10158

Routledge is an imprint of the Taylor & Francis Group, an informa business

British Library Cataloguing-in-Publication Data
A catalogue record for this book is available from the British Library

ISBN: 978-1-032-41060-9 (hbk)
ISBN: 978-1-032-41061-6 (pbk)
ISBN: 978-1-003-35605-9 (ebk)

DOI: 10.4324/9781003356059

Typeset in Times New Roman
by Newgen Publishing UK

Contents

List of contributors *vii*

Introduction 1
KATARZYNA PIWOWAR-SULEJ AND MARIUSZ SOŁTYSIK

1 Agile, complexity and sustainability in project management: A preliminary ordering of the research area 5
CZESŁAW MESJASZ AND TOMASZ MAŁKUS

2 Integrating sustainability and project success: A stakeholder value approach 35
EWA SOŃTA-DRĄCZKOWSKA

3 The role of sustainable dynamics in organizational transformation and project success 50
SZYMON CYFERT AND MACIEJ ZASTEMPOWSKI

4 Sustainable project management by considering the impact of modern technologies on stakeholder management 73
SEWERYN SPAŁEK

5 Sustainable project management in nonprofit organizations: Research results from Poland 87
ANNA MARCISZEWSKA, RENATA BRAJER-MARCZAK AND ANNA ZABŁOCKA-KLUCZKA

6 The evolution of project managers' competencies and leadership styles: The agility and sustainability contexts 108
KATARZYNA GRZESIK AND KATARZYNA PIWOWAR-SULEJ

7 Team members' competencies in sustainable project management 126
MAŁGORZATA TYRAŃSKA, SYLWIA WIŚNIEWSKA, AND ROBERT SZYDŁO

Index *137*

Contributors

Renata Brajer-Marczak, PhD, DSc, is currently working as an Associate Professor in the Department of Economics and Organization of Enterprises, Faculty of Management, at the Wroclaw University of Economics and Business, Poland. Her scientific interests include business process management and project management. In particular, her current research interests focus on the green business process management, business process improvement, nonprofit organizations and sustainable project management of organizations.

Szymon Cyfert is the Head of the Department of Organization and Management Theory at the Poznan University of Economics, Poland. He is a member of the Scientific Excellence Council, as well as the Organization and Management Committee at the Polish Academy of Sciences. His research interests include organization excellence, strategic management, and organization and management theory.

Katarzyna Grzesik, PhD, is an Assistant Professor in the Department of Economics and Organization of Enterprises at the Wroclaw University of Economics and Business, Poland. Her research interests focus on leadership in an organization, human resource management and decision-making in an organization. She is the author of more than 50 publications in these areas. She is a university lecturer, academic tutor and the head of the postgraduate program Psychology in Management at the Wroclaw University of Economics and Business.

Tomasz Małkus is Assistant Professor in the Management Process Department at Cracow University of Economics,, Poland. His research interests include logistics, project management, particularly R&D and innovative projects in the area of logistics and IT support of enterprise management, and assessment of EU-funded projects. He coordinates with the Małopolska (Kraków Region) Regional Group International Project Management Association and is a member of the Polish Logistics Association and Logistics Guild at the Technical University of Kosice (Slovakia).

Anna Marciszewska, PhD, DSc, is currently working as an Associate Professor in the Department of Economics and Organization of Enterprises, Faculty of

Management, at the Wroclaw University of Economics and Business, Poland. Her scientific interests focus on project management methods and techniques, including EU projects. She specializes in issues of project management in nonprofit organizations. Her latest research is devoted to the issues of project maturity in nonprofit organizations, process improvement and sustainable project management of organizations.

Czesław Mesjasz is Associate Professor in the Management Process Department at Cracow University of Economics, Poland. His research interests include management theory, systems approach, including complexity science, conflict and negotiation, project management and corporate governance. He has also been in long-term cooperation with international systems research community, and is a member of international professional organizations including Academy of Management, International Sociological Association (Research Committee 51 on Sociocybernetics).

Katarzyna Piwowar-Sulej is Full Professor and is currently working at the Faculty of Business and Management, Wroclaw University of Economics and Business, Poland. Her research interests are sustainable human resource management, sustainable leadership, and agile and sustainable project management. She is an experienced HR manager and project manager (in terms of HR and research projects). She is also a winner of two scholarship competitions financed by the European Social Fund. She is the author of more than 180 publications and participant of more than 60 conferences as a lecturer or expert. She is an active reviewer with publishers such as Elsevier, Emerald and Springer. In 2023 she was awarded by Wiley for a top-downloaded article and by Emerald for an outstanding paper and reviews.

Mariusz Sołtysik is a Professor in the College of Management and Quality Sciences at the University of Economics, Krakow. He is vice-chairman of the Małopolska Regional Group of the International Project Management Association and coordinator of implementation works in the Strategic Program of Scientific Research and Development Works. He is also a contractor in projects financed by the National Science Center and the National Center for Research and Development, including the Lider program. He was the contractor of the H2020-EU program 3.2.4.3. He is a scientific leader of the research on the complexity of managing organizations in the fourth industrial revolution in the project entitled "Social-economic Consequences of the Fourth Industrial Revolution", where he deals with the issue of the human–machine relationship.

Ewa Sońta-Drączkowska is Assistant Professor at the Department of Project Management, Management Institute, College of Management and Finance, SGH. She is an experienced project management practitioner, trainer, and academic lecturer. She specializes in project management, translating strategy into actions, managing in a multi-project environment, leading teams and people in projects. She is the mentor for Enactus, an organization implementing social innovations. She is the author of numerous publications and a speaker at national and international conferences.

Seweryn Spałek, PhD, MSc, ICT-Eng, is Full Professor of Business and Management at the Silesian University of Technology, Poland. He possesses extensive knowledge and expertise in business and project management, both in theory and practice. Since 1994, he has advised and managed several business and IT projects in companies and healthcare organizations, in multicultural and multinational environments. Moreover, he is the author and coauthor of several publications. He has additionally participated as a speaker in several conferences related to business and project management (e.g., at the Project Management Institute Global Congresses [Europe, North America and Australia]; University of California, Berkley; University of Cambridge, England) and has been a lecturer of MBA and postgraduate studies. Finally, he is a member of the Academy Of Management, Project Management Institute and International Project Management Association.

Robert Szydło is a human resource management specialist and psychologist in the Department of Labor Resource Management, Krakow University of Economics. He is interested in employability, competence development, gamification, and the usage of psychology in business. He is engaged in various scientific, didactic and voluntary activities and is a leader of the science-based NGO and SEED Association.

Małgorzata Tyrańska is an Associate Professor at the Cracow University of Economics, Poland, with a postdoctoral degree in economic science in the discipline of management sciences. Her research interests include employment restructuring, organizational structure improvement, job evaluation, competency profile assessment and employee evaluation. Since 2015 she is a member of the experts' team for the evaluation of projects implemented as part of European programs.

Sylwia Wiśniewska, PhD in economics in the discipline of management sciences, is an Assistant Professor at the Department of Labor Resources Management at Cracow University of Economics, Poland. Her research interests include employability, sustainable employability, competencies and quality of life. She collaborates with business practices, including nongovernmental organizations, as an expert.

Anna Zabłocka-Kluczka, PhD Eng, is currently working as an Assistant Professor in the Department of Management Systems and Organizational Development, Faculty of Management, at Wroclaw University of Science and Technology, Poland. Her scientific interests focus on management concepts, methods and techniques (in particular controlling, change management, crisis management and business continuity management). Her latest research is devoted to the issues of organizational resilience and reliability, and sustainable functioning of organizations.

Maciej Zastempowski heads the Department of Enterprise Management at Nicolaus Copernicus University, Poland. He is a member of the Organization and Management Sciences Committee at the Polish Academy of Sciences and the International Joseph A. Schumpeter Society. His research interests include innovative management in contemporary organizations.

Introduction

Katarzyna Piwowar-Sulej and Mariusz Sołtysik

The first literature addressing sustainability can be traced as early as in 1713 regarding the sustainability of forests in terms of logging regrown timber alone to retain soil fertility. Nowadays sustainable development is defined taking into account the Triple Bottom Line (TBL) framework (people, planet, profit). Moreover, this concept is still being developed, transferring to organizational level (Baumgartner and Ebner, 2010; Dyllick and Muff, 2016) and different theoretical/practical domains such as project management (PM) (Armenia *et al.*, 2019; Chawla *et al.*, 2018).

Sustainable PM can be defined as

> planning, monitoring and controlling the processes of project implementation and support, taking into account the environmental, economic and social aspects of the life cycle of resources, processes, products and project effects, aimed at achieving benefits for stakeholders and carried out in a transparent, fair manner and an ethical way that involves the proactive participation of stakeholders
>
> (Silvius and Schipper, 2014)

Sustainable PM is called a new school of management thought that emphasizes that sustainability may be incorporated into a project lifecycle (sustainability in projects) and can be a result of projects (sustainability through projects). Sustainable PM is also a growing trend visible in the publications discussing PM (Wawak and Woźniak, 2020). These publications address sustainability issues mainly in construction and development projects because such types of projects utilize a significant amount of resources that have the potential to negatively influence the environment (Deland, 2009; Labuschagne *et al.*, 2005). If sustainable project performance measures are created, they also refer mainly to the abovementioned types of projects (e.g., Liu *et al.*, 2021; Sanmi and Ayodeji, 2019). The discussion about sustainability in these projects is directed toward the environmental bottom line. However, in other types of projects the full assumptions of sustainability can be implemented that requires balancing of economic, environmental, and social aspects (Zakrzewska *et al.*, 2022). Moreover, although projects can be performed in line with different PM methodologies, there is scarcity of research on

DOI: 10.4324/9781003356059-1

the linkage between individual PM methodologies and sustainability in projects. Only a few studies show that agile project management (APM) framework meets the assumptions of sustainable development (Zakrzewska *et al.*, 2022). Finally, the issue of competencies needed for sustainable PM is also a neglected area of research. Silvius and Schipper (2014) emphasized the competency gap of project managers. Other authors (such as Al-Qassab *et al.* (2019)) focused only on managers' competencies for green project. Such issues as the linkage between agile and sustainable competencies and competencies needed from project team members have not been covered by research.

The main goal of the monograph will be to fill the gap presented above through the theoretical and empirical research of APM's connections with the assumptions of sustainable development. In addition, the linkage between PM methodologies and project sustainability will be identified. The identification will be based on the aspects of the impact of sustainable PM on the transformation of companies toward sustainable development.

The book resulting from our project has three equally important goals. The first goal is to identify and assess the validity of the application of the concepts of sustainable development in the family of agile methodological frameworks. The second goal is to use the research results as an introduction to further in-depth research focused on the future relationship between the ideas of sustainable development and APM. The third goal is to identify the competencies that are needed to successfully implement projects in the context of sustainable development.

The book consists of seven chapters. The first, titled "Agile, Complexity and Sustainability in Project Management: A Preliminary Ordering of the Research Area," explores the linguistic inconsistencies in the contemporary PM literature, with a particular focus on sustainability, agility, and complexity. It provides a theoretical framework that highlights the crucial role of effective communication in handling these concepts.

In Chapter 2, titled "Integrating Sustainability and Project Success: A Stakeholder Value Approach," the integration of sustainability and project success is explored, with a focus on the application of stakeholder theory as the foundational framework. Traditional approaches to measuring project success are reviewed, and the incorporation of sustainability into project goals is discussed, proposing an expanded perspective using the Sustainable Balance Scorecard (SCBS). Emerging trends in sustainable PM, including the synergy between APM and sustainability, are identified.

Chapter 3, "The Role of Sustainable Dynamics in Organizational Transformation and Project Success," investigates how Sustainable Dynamic Abilities (SDA) impact organizational transformation and project success, specifically in terms of environmental orientation and project outcomes. Empirical research suggests that SDA positively influence internal environmental orientation but have an ambiguous impact on external environmental orientation, affecting only certain aspects of project success.

In the following chapter, "Sustainable Project Management by Considering the Impact of Modern Technologies on Stakeholder Management," the influence of modern technologies on PM, particularly in the contexts of sustainability and agility, is discussed. The chapter focuses on the analysis of technological factors' impact on stakeholder management in projects, based on global empirical research in enterprises.

Chapter 5, titled "Sustainable Project Management in Nonprofit Organizations: Research Results from Poland," aims to fill research gaps in sustainable PM practices and methodologies applied in nonprofit organizations. Results from theoretical and empirical research are presented, including the frequency of sustainable PM practices in nonprofit organizations compared to business organizations.

Chapter 6, "The Evolution of Project Managers' Competencies and Leadership Styles—The Agility and Sustainability Contexts," examines project manager competencies in traditional, agile, and sustainable PM contexts, highlighting inconsistencies in competency profiles. Leadership styles in PM are also discussed, including the adoption of Management 3.0 and sustainable leadership concepts.

The final chapter, "Team Members' Competencies in Sustainable Project Management" provides characteristics of work in projects and analyzes different frameworks related to competencies required from project team members in terms of sustainable PM. It also synthesizes the knowledge on competencies that are the most frequently shown in the literature.

References

Al-Qassab, H. et al. (2019) "Sustainability and Green Project Management Skills: An Exploratory Study in the Construction Industry in Dubai'" in Leal, F. W. (ed.) *Social Responsibility and Sustainability*. Cham: Springer, pp. 223–239. doi: 10.1007/978-3-030-03562-4_12

Armenia, S. et al. (2019) "Sustainable project management: A conceptualization-oriented review and a framework proposal for future studies", *Sustainability*, 11(9), p. 2664. doi: 10.3390/su11092664.

Baumgartner, R. J. and Ebner, D. (2010) "Corporate sustainability strategies: sustainability profiles and maturity levels", *Sustainable Development*, 18(2), pp. 76–89. doi: 10.1002/sd.447

Chawla, V. K. et al. (2018) 'The sustainable project management: A review and future possibilities', *Journal of Project Management*, pp. 157–170. doi: 10.5267/j.jpm.2018.2.001.

Deland, D. (2009) "Sustainability through project management and net impact", in PMI® Global Congress 2009. Orlando: Project Management Institute. Available at: www.pmi.org/learning/library/sustainability-goals-achieving-framework-technique-6776

Dyllick, T. and Muff, K. (2016) "Clarifying the meaning of sustainable business", *Organization & Environment*, 29(2), pp. 156–174. doi: 10.1177/1086026615575176

Labuschagne, C., Brent, A. C. and van Erck, R. P. G. (2005) "Assessing the sustainability performances of industries", *Journal of Cleaner Production*, 13(4), pp. 373–385. doi: 10.1016/j.jclepro.2003.10.007

Liu, M. et al. (2021) "Risk-based metanetwork modeling for sustainable project performance in international construction', *Journal of Infrastructure Systems*, 27(3), p. 04021020. doi: 10.1061/(ASCE)IS.1943-555X.0000617

Sanmi, O. and Ayodeji, O. (2019) "Criteria for measuring sustainable construction project performance in Nigeria", *IOP Conference Series: Earth and Environmental Science*, 331(1), p. 012020. doi: 10.1088/1755-1315/331/1/012020

Silvius, A. J. G. and Schipper, R. P. J. (2014) "Sustainability in project management: A literature review and impact analysis", *Social Business*, 4(1), pp. 63–96. doi: 10.1362/204440814X13948909253866

Wawak, S. and Woźniak, K. (2020) "Evolution of project management studies in the XXI century", *International Journal of Managing Projects in Business*, 13(4), pp. 867–888. doi: 10.1108/IJMPB-01-2020-0002

Zakrzewska, M. et al. (2022) "The linkage between Agile project management and sustainable development: A theoretical and empirical view", *Sustainable Development*. doi: 10.1002/sd.2285

1 Agile, complexity and sustainability in project management

A preliminary ordering of the research area

Czesław Mesjasz and Tomasz Małkus

Introduction to the problem

One of the specific characteristics of modern management, and subsequently project management, is the application of polysemous terms, i.e., concepts having multiple meanings. Sustainability and the concepts of agile and agility can be used as examples.

Focusing attention on project management, and referring to management whenever necessary, it must be emphasized that this linguistic point of view is not incidental but it responds to new challenges for project management, especially deriving from the global and local environmental changes that have become one of the biggest problems in project management area of human activities.

Because various kinds of projects are complex by themselves and they are realized under complex circumstances, that is why complexity has become a natural attribute of modern project management. Additionally, since the 1990s, the applications of variously defined ideas referring to agile and agility have begun to exert their influence on project management. As a result sustainability, agile and complexity have to be considered more often jointly in multiple areas of project management. Until now, only preliminary studies dealing with that problem can be quoted (Silvius *et al.* 2016; Dong *et al.* 2021).

Leaving apart the above pioneering works, it can be observed that agile, complexity and sustainability are applied without a necessary profound conceptual reflection or they are presented in such a way that their meaning must be defined separately for the use in specific applications. It also has to be added that due to its polysemous character, each of these terms can become a void slogan, if not a "buzzword".

The lack of more precise interpretations, especially in the case of sustainability, is incorrectly compensated by the claims about urgency of the problems. Taking into account that these three terms often must be applied together makes the situation in project management significantly intricate.

A question arises as to what can be done under such circumstances as not to become lost in imprecisely defined and confusing terminology that in consequence may lead to low-quality theoretical considerations and practical applications.

DOI: 10.4324/9781003356059-2

Before developing the conceptual framework helpful in studying and performing the projects in which sustainability, complexity and agile constitute indispensable characteristics, it is necessary to remind that communication allowing for an effective transfer of meaning constitutes the foundation of theoretical considerations and practical activities.

The main aim of this chapter is to propose a conceptual framework for developing all types of projects and project management processes in which the challenges deriving from sustainability must be dealt with the applications of ideas taken from complexity-related studies and agile-related ideas. This aim can be divided into the following partial aims:

1 Identification of interpretations of agile and complexity in project management.
2 Identification of relations between project management, projects and sustainability.
3 Development of an introductory conceptual methodological framework applicable in the situations when sustainability in projects and project management increases complexity of the problems and when the use of agile and agility is necessary.

The preliminary character of the research does not require more profound computer-supported studies of the literature. On contrary, any forms of meta-analysis of literature used as the main research methods in the studies of the polysemous concepts can be misleading due to multitude and variety of interpretations. Therefore an introductory survey of interpretations of such terms is essential for further, more refined and methodologically advanced investigations of literature sources.

The chapter is not designed as a profound specialist linguistic and hermeneutic study. It is developed from the perspective of theory and practice of project management. It is only showing in an introductory way how the consequences of a polysemous character of agile, complexity and sustainability should be dealt with in modern project management.

Two terminological explanations must be added. First, in most cases the main object of discussion is project management. It is neglected, purposively or not, that characteristics of projects should be sometimes separated from characteristics of the process of project management. This divide is significant in the case of agile project management frameworks and agile projects. In the case of complexity it is rather evident that complexity in project management is inseparable from complexity of projects. Separation of sustainability in project management, especially in its processual interpretation, and sustainability of projects is necessary, although a precise disassociation is not always achievable.

Second, in the discussions on project management, the term "agile" is accompanied by the term "agility". Sometimes Agile is treated as a proper name. Wherever necessary the differences of meaning of these three notions are explained.

The remainder of the chapter is organized into six parts. In the first part, a collection of problems deriving from applications of polysemous terms in project management theory and practice is described. In the second part, a survey of interpretations of the term Agile in management and project management is presented. The third part includes an attempt to order the interpretations of complexity-related ideas. In the fourth part, a preliminary survey of terminological problems associated with sustainability in management is developed. In the fifth part, a similar survey of sustainability in projects and project management is presented. The sixth part includes a methodological conceptual framework of applications of Agile methodological frameworks and complexity-related concepts in sustainability-related project management.

The polysemous terms in project management: Agile, complexity and sustainability

Some specific characteristics of modern social studies, including management and process management, are the consequences of the following linguistic phenomena:

- Polysemy, i.e., number and multiplicity of meanings
- Polysemy frequently accompanied by imprecise fundamental, initial definitions (interpretations)
- Fuzzy and overlapping ranges of multiple meanings

Polysemy is the phenomenon whereby a single word form is associated with two or several related senses. It is distinguished from monosemy, where one word form is associated with a single meaning, and homonymy, where a single word form is associated with two or several unrelated meanings (Vicente and Falkum 2017, pp. 1–3).

When studying polysemy, the distinction between ambiguity and vagueness also must be borne in mind. It was described by Tuggy (1993, p. 273): "The difference between ambiguity and vagueness is a matter of whether two or more meanings associated with a given phonological form are distinct (ambiguous), or united as non-distinguished subcases of a single, more general meaning (vague)". A standard example is bank "financial institution" vs. bank "land at river edge", where the meanings are intuitively quite separate; in aunt "father's sister" vs. aunt "mother's sister", however, the meanings are intuitively united into one, "parent's sister". Thus ambiguity corresponds to separation, and vagueness to unity, of different meanings.

Incidentally, the discussion on the interpretations of agile in software development brought about an observation that is connected to polysemy, fuzziness and overlapping ranges of meanings. Fowler, a software development blogger, without referring to any deeper linguistic phenomena proposed the term semantic diffusion as reflecting the evolution and spread of the meaning of the terms that are initially relatively well-defined. According to Fowler (2006):

> Semantic diffusion occurs when you have a word that is coined by a person or group, often with a pretty good definition, but then gets spread through the

wider community in a way that weakens that definition. This weakening risks losing the definition entirely – and with it any usefulness to the term.

Fowler treated semantic diffusion as a neologism, and as an example he used the term agile. In the light of the above considerations, the precision of initial definitions and interpretations of agile is not so unequivocal. It can be added that agile since its origins was not interpreted clearly. The scope of the meaning of this term and fuzziness of borders of that scope of meaning constitute the fundamental challenge in defining agile and agility in management and project management.

Kiklewicz (2006a, pp. 20-21) developed and applied a more formal definition: "The semantic diffusion is defined as non-determining of the content of linguistic signs (morphemes, words, word groups, sentences, texts), the indistinct character of borders between semantic categories in the system of language as well as in the linguistic communication". It can be concluded that semantic diffusions relate to the scope of meaning and its borders. Polysemy and semantic diffusion occur parallelly in creating meanings predominantly by metonymies and metaphors. These brief interpretations of polysemy, semantic diffusion and their relations are only recalled as a potential direction for further studies and as a source of a more profound reflection in the remaining part of this study. As preliminary sources for such studies, the following works can be recommended: Lakoff and Johnson (1980/1995), Ortony (1993) and Steen (2017).

Applications of polysemous utterances with a broad scope of meaning with not too precisely defined meaning have three fundamental sources and multiple consequences in the studies of society. The first one is the extension of philosophical foundations beyond positivism and neo-positivism predominantly caused by the emergence of constructivism, postmodernism and post-structuralism. The second cause is a growing need for more profound hermeneutical studies. Subsequently, the third cause is the need to develop more advanced linguistic considerations.

The above causes have the following theoretical and practical consequences. First, the polysemous, fuzzily defined terms create significant problems in assigning more specific meaning for qualitative narratives. Second, they create significant barriers for operationalization (Bridgman 1955) and measurement deriving from operationism (Stevens 1968). Third, the effectiveness of the communication process based on such notions is diminished. Finally, since the action is always conditioned by communication and transfer of meaning, the terms with multiple, broad imprecise meaning may lead to a decreasing effectiveness of activities in the areas where they are applied.

The emerging divide between positivist vs. interpretive approach in theory of management was described by Burrell and Morgan in their book published for the first time in 1979 and then reprinted multiple times (Burrell and Morgan 1998). In their book they identified four paradigms of social studies, also relevant to management and project management: radical humanist, radical structuralist, interpretive and functionalist (Burrell and Morgan 1998, p. 22). Without delving into the subtleties and differences among those paradigms, we can consider a dualist approach – interpretive and constructivist, including the role of the observer vs.

objective, objectivist and positivist in which the object of studies is independent from the observer. This universal problem is especially important when the role of the observer is discussed in the research on complexity in management and project management (Gell-Mann 1994, p. 33; Stacey *et al.* 2000; Mesjasz *et al.* 2022).

One of the consequences of the emergence of those paradigms is the problem of definitions of the fundamental terms. In the simplified way these consequences for both fundamental paradigms that can be called as subjectivist/constructivist and objectivist/positivist are described in the following paragraph.

It is commonly agreed that social entities are social constructs (Berger and Luckmann 1966; Searle 1995). Subsequently, in the subjectivist and interpretative approaches the final meaning of terms is created in as an intersubjective idea in the communication process (Leydesdorff 2011). Additionally, operationalization and operationist approach are not given sufficient weight in the language games. Therefore it was and it is somehow natural that the strive for classical definitions had to give ground for a semantically more liberal approach. Agreeing with a constructive character of social entities, it is accepted that the meaning of the terms can be made more precise in the process of discourse.

The broad and fuzzy scope of meaning of the polysemous terms used in all areas of social sciences, including management and project management, brings about the following consequences:

1 Limited possibility to create meaning in intersubjective discourse.
2 Lowering of effective communication. The communication is effective when the parts involved in the interaction create the meaning that is similar (not identical).
3 In consequence of lowered effective communication, due to the link between mind and action, the effectiveness of generally depicted actions and their circumstances can also decrease.
4 The polysemous, broadly and fuzzily defined terms create problems for positivist approach when the problems of measurement, operationalization and operationism are emerging.
5 The terms with a polysemous, broad and fuzzy scope of meaning could also be the cause for a negative impact of political power on constructing the meaning.
6 The polysemous and fuzzily defined terms with a broad scope of meaning may also have an impact on the performative aspects of discourse (Austin 1962; Searle 1995).
7 The abovementioned terms can also create obstacles in education. The teachers and the learners must spent more time and efforts to create mutual understanding.
8 There may be problems deriving from scaling. Agile and agility in a relatively small software development project have a different meaning than agile in a multilevel large scale project. The problem of scaling has also a significant importance in the discussions on sustainability.
9 Specific problems occur when the polysemous terms with a fuzzy and broad scope of meaning are treated as persuasive utterances (Sopory and Dillard

2002). In addition to the precision in defining the meaning, specific additional measures have to be undertaken as to use the arguments allowing to change the state of mind of the persuaded actors.

When studying the relations between agile, complexity and sustainability, all the abovementioned problems have to be considered. For each term the situation is different. In this preliminary study all those terms are given attention from a perspective of the above characteristics. Obviously, it is just the first step in more advanced research.

Agile in management

Undoubtedly agile and agility have become a collection of the most frequently used terms in management and project management. Before further considerations, a terminological explanation is necessary. As polysemous terms, they have many definitions and interpretations. In this chapter only the genesis of these concepts and selected representative samples of definitions and interpretations are presented.

The adjective agile and the noun agility were introduced in management already in the 1980s (Brown and Agnew 1982) and the 1990s. Agile in project management originated in the 1990s. Agile as a proper name of a methodological framework was initially associated with software development (Manifesto for Agile Software Development, 2001), and later it was transferred to other areas of project management and management (Highsmith 2000, 2002, 2010). At present the utterances agile, agility and Agile are often used interchangeably in management and project management, making the efforts of deeper analysis of their meaning difficult, if possible at all.

An etymological analysis is always useful in terminological discussions. It is then worthwhile to remind that the term agile, meaning having quickness of motion, nimble, active (of body or mind), derives from the French agile and directly from the Latin *agilis*, "nimble, quick" (*Online Etymology Dictionary*, www.etymonline.com). *Merriam-Webster* defines agile as: 1: Marked by ready ability to move with quick easy grace, e.g., an agile dancer; 2: having a quick resourceful and adaptable character, e.g., an agile mind (www.merriam-webster.com/dictionary/).

In the discussion on the applications of the notions agile and agility in management, the following issues have to be addressed:

- Origins of applications of agile and agility in management
- Polysemy of agile and agility in management

Origins of applications of agile and agility in management

Brown and Agnew (1982, p. 29) were the first to define the concept of *corporate agility* as "... the capacity to react quickly to rapidly changing circumstances, requires a focus on clear system output goals and the capability to match human resources to the demands of changing circumstances".

A significant influence on the introduction of the concepts of agile and agility in management was exerted by the book published by Dertouzos *et al.* (1989). This book, based on a report by a team of specialists from the Massachusetts Institute of Technology, states that the US economy must change significantly to meet the demands of competitiveness. This report formed the basis of another report prepared at the Iacocca Institute at Lehigh University (Nagel 1992). This report introduces the concept of *agile manufacturing*. It has the following features (Nagel 1992, pp. 7–8):

- Products are custom-designed and configured at the time of order
- Products can be reconfigured and upgraded to meet evolving requirements
- Product life can be extended and the value of distinct product generations can be reduced
- Long-term relationships can be established with customers who are committed to the evolving products they use and to the companies that maintain the currency of those products

Rapid product creation, development and modification in an agile manufacturing enterprise is made possible by

- the routine formation of interdisciplinary project teams able to develop product designs and manufacturing process specifications concurrently,
- extending the concept of design to the entire projected life cycle of a product, from initial specifications to its eventual disposal,
- the availability of scientific knowledge of the manufacturing process, of computers capable of accurately simulating product performance characteristics and of modeling the entire manufacturing process,
- modular, flexible, reconfigurable, affordable production processes and equipment,
- the ability to obtain relevant information quickly, to share it with project members distributed throughout a firm and in different firms, and to link that information directly to production machinery, and
- modular product design incorporating reconfigurability and upgradability leading to extremely long product lifetimes.

A strong impact on the creation and propagation of the concept *of agile manufacturing* was exerted by a book (Goldman *et al.*, 1995), with a foreword by Lee Iaccoca. In this book, the authors treat agility as a fundamental characteristic of an enterprise regarding marketing, production, design, organization and management, and people. They provided the following definition of management agility, which many authors also treat as basic (Goldman *et al.*, 1995, p. 42):

> Agility is dynamic, context-specific, aggressively change-embracing and growth-oriented. It is not about improving efficiency, cutting costs, or battening down the business hatches to ride out fearsome competitive "storms". It is

> about succeeding and about winning: about succeeding in emerging competitive arenas, and about winning profits market share, and customers in the very center of the competitive storms many companies now fear.

Polysemy of agile and agility in management

In the second half of 1990s, multiple interpretations of agile and agility followed the initial concepts.

A synthesis of agile manufacturing interpretations was presented by Gunasekaran (1998, 1999). As a starting point, he considers the following general characteristics (dimensions) of an agile manufacturing enterprise (Gunasekaran 1998, p. 1223):

- Value-based pricing strategies that enrich customers
- Cooperation that enhances competitiveness
- Organizational mastery of change and uncertainty
- Investments that leverage the impact of people and information

Agility described in this way is based on four underlying principles: delivering value to the customers, being ready for change, valuing human knowledge and skills, and forming virtual partnerships. Gunasekaran (1998, p. 1226) also emphasized the role of the innovative way of operating an agile enterprise in all areas of its activity, namely marketing, design and production, organization and management, and people.

In another study, Gunasekaran (1999, p. 89) distinguished the basic areas of agile manufacturing:

1 Strategies: virtual enterprise, supply chain, concurrent engineering
2 Technologies: hardware – tools and equipment – and information technology
3 Systems: design systems, production planning and control systems, system integration and database management
4 People: top management support and employee empowerment, training and education

In the discussion on agile and agility in management, other attempts were made to organize the reference areas of applications of these terms. Kettunen (2009, pp. 26–27) identified agility in the following business areas: strategic agility, business agility, enterprise agility, agile organization, agile workforce, IT agility, agile manufacturing and agile supply chain.

Based on a preliminary review of selected basic papers published in English and review papers, e.g., Kim Schirrmacher and Schopp (2018), a set of various terms describing the reference objects of agile and agility applied by different authors should be distinguished (see the examples listed below). Additionally, attention must be paid to the terminological problems existing in the English language concerning the terms “company”, “enterprise”, “corporation” and “corporate”.

These terminological problems concerning the interpretations of the objects of research are usually neglected but in the case of more profound terminological considerations their role should be scrutinized more profoundly.

1 Agile manufacturing – in some interpretations, agile manufacturing is treated as a superior concept in relation to other concepts (Nagel 1992; Goldman *et al.*, 1995; Gunasekaran 1998, 1999)
2 Agile manufacturing enterprise (Dove 1991; Nagel 1992; Gunasekaran 1998, 1999)
3 Agile enterprise (Dove 1991; Nagel 1992; Gunasekaran 1998, 1999).
4 Corporate agility (Brown and Agnew 1982, p. 29)
5 Agile organization (Gunasekaran 1998, 1999)
6 Organizational agility (Dove 1999)

In studies from the 1990s to the 20th century, *agility* was associated with the flexibility of manufacturing systems. Duguay *et al.* (1997, p. 1188) selected the following definition from multiple sources: "Applied to the industrial context, flexibility is the capacity to deploy or redeploy production resources efficiently as required by changes in the environment". They take agility and flexibility together. They point out that *agility* is the ability to quickly adapt not only to fluctuations in demand but also to many other changes in its environment.

A similar interpretation was presented by Tan (1998, p. 376): "Agility and flexibility are closely related. In its most restricted form flexibility refers to adaptability and versatility while agility is related to the speed that a system adapts. Therefore flexibility is a necessary condition for agility".

Another distinction between agility and flexibility of the enterprise was shown by Baker (1996). As a basis for the distinction, he took the level of hierarchy at which they occur in the organization. Agility is about the strategic level, whereas flexibility is about the operational level. To achieve agility at the organizational and network level of an organization, flexibility is needed at the operational level.

The common understanding of agility in management and project management was also studied by the Project Management Institute. The following practices of organizational agility were distinguished and used as the foundation of empirical research (Project Management Institute 2012, p. 3): quick response to strategic opportunities, shorter decision/production/review cycles, focus on change management, integrating voice of the customer, focus on risk management, interdisciplinary project teams, elimination of organization silos, contingency planning, use of iterative project management practices and leveraging technology.

The above unordered collection of various interpretations of the terms agile and agility in broadly defined management reflects a great variety of sources of these terms and of their interpretations. It also confirms the earlier discussion about limited possibilities of developing more precise and nonintuitive interpretations of agile and agility in management deriving from their polysemous character.

Agile and agility in project management

The introduction of agile and agility concepts in project management was initiated in software development. The development of agile and agility in this area of project management can be divided into two periods – before and after the declaration of the Manifesto for Agile Software Development (2001).

For the first time, the agility in software development was proposed by Aoyama in the Agile Software Process (ASP) methodological approach. The ASP aimed to develop software quickly while maintaining the flexibility needed to respond to changing requirements. At the same time, due to complexity and vulnerability to disruption of the ASP, higher than conventional software process models, it had to operate within a specially tailored software engineering environment to function smoothly. Aoyama and his team at Fujitsu developed two key methods among various management – the time-based process inaction model and just-in-time process management (Aoyama 1998, p. 57). In a synthetic description, the ASP placed emphasis on rapid and flexible adaptation to changes in process, product and environment. It is characterized by three core processes: incremental and evolutionary process, modular and lean process, and time-based process. In Fujitsu, where ASP was used for the development of large-scale communication systems, the ASP was operationalized through the use of a network-centric tools designed for the agile software engineering environment (Aoyama 1998; Abrahamsson *et al.* 2010, pp. 33–34).

The importance of agile and agility in software development gained momentum after the historic meeting of 17 software development specialists at Snowbird Ski Resort in the Wasatch Mountains of Utah from 11 to 13 February 2001. Among them were the authors of the following methods: Scrum, Dynamic Systems Development Method (DSDM), Crystal Methods, Feature-Driven Development (FDD), Extreme Programming (XP) and Adaptive Software Development (ASD) (Highsmith 2002, p. vii; Cockburn 2007, p. 655). During this meeting, the Agile Alliance was created, and the meaning of Agile postulates (proper noun) was formulated in the *Manifesto for Agile Software Development* (2001) and the *Principles behind the Agile Manifesto* (2001).

The importance of Agile in software development can be further understood by Cockburn's description of the circumstances of the Manifesto (2007, pp. 654–660). It is especially worth reading the discussion on agile vs. adaptive and precision comprehension levels. Additional light on the interpretation of agile in project management can be shed when recalling some interesting aspects of creating the term during the meeting in Utah (Rigby *et al.* 2016). They draw attention to two facts. The proposal to call the new approach in software development agile arose from the fact that one of the participants of the meeting (the authors do not specify which) was reading a book at the time (Goldman *et al.* 1995). In addition, they reminded that although the concept of *agile* dominates in project management, its genesis should be sought in management.

It is not our aim to extract the interpretations of Agile from these two well-known documents. In order to study the meaning of agile, agility and Agile in project management, it is worthwhile to answer the following question: What were the interpretations of agile and agility proposed by the specialists who proclaimed the Manifesto? In this case a chronological approach seems relevant.

First and foremost it can be observed that there were not any attempts to define agile and agility in software development, except the one already mentioned by Aoyama (1998), before the meeting announcing the Agile Manifesto (2001). In the following year a number of attempts of defining agile and agility in software development were made. In the broadest sense, Agile (as a proper name) in project management was defined by Cockburn and Highsmith. In September 2001 they published a paper in which they presented the ideas of Agile developed earlier in February 2001 (Highsmith and Cockburn 2001).

The proper name Agile is predominantly associated with the software development and subsequently in the project management in a universal sense. In the sense used in the Agile Manifesto and the *Principles behind the Agile Manifesto*, Agile can be treated as a broad methodological framework (approach) applied in specific solutions in the software development. It was also extended by the Project Management Institute treating agile (with lowercase character) as a methodological framework (Agile Practice Guide 2017) and agility as features of objects and processes that are linked to management and project management in the general sense.

An interesting relation between agility in business management and project management was recalled by Highsmith. In his book surveying the origins of Agile project management, he referred to the definition of agility in management proposed by Goldman *et al.* (1995, p. 5): "Agility … is a comprehensive response to the business challenges of profiting from rapidly changing, continually fragmenting, global markets for high-quality, high performance, customer-configured goods and services".

This quotation includes another interpretation of agility and also confirms a strong impact of agility developed in business management on agility in software development at the time of establishing the concept of Agile.

In the studies of the origins of the concept of Agile, a priority must be given to the pioneering role of Highsmith, due to the scope of depth of contributions visible in his publications (Highsmith 2000, 2002, 2010; Highsmith and Cockburn 2001). In the early period of development of agile it was defined and described by Highsmith (2002) in several ways.

The favorite definition of agility of Highsmith was formulated as follows: "… the ability to both create and respond to change in order to profit in a turbulent business environment" (2002, p. X). Other characteristics of agility were also enumerated in that book: (a) "… three other components that help define agility: nimbleness and improvisation, conformance to actual, and balancing flexibility and structure" (p. 16); (b) "Ability to juggle and improvise" (p. 17); (c) "Agile requires discipline and skill" (p. 17); (d) "Agile individuals are able to improvise … in today's turbulent environment, staff members with good balancing, judging, and improvisational skills are truly invaluable" (p. 17); (e) "Agile projects are not controlled by conformance to plan but by conformance to business value" (p. 17) and (f) "Agile allows balancing flexibility and structure ... operating with flexibly followed set of rules ... without the rules... . Without some rule set, however, agility can become rudderless reaction" (p. 18).

The above characteristics assigned by Highsmith initially to software development and project management were later extended to management. In the book published later, Highsmith (2010) extended the above ideas from project management to management in a universal sense.

The detailed analysis of all attributes of agile, agility and Agile presented by some of the authors of the Agile Manifesto remain beyond the scope of this study. Here they are recalled as to show how differentiated, unordered and random were the first efforts to produce interpretations of Agile, agile and agility in project management. They were surveyed in the first decade of the 20th century, the era of rapid development and expansion of Agile to project management treated in a more universal sense (Kettunen 2009; Abrahamsson *et al.* 2010; Conforto *et al.* 2014).

Complexity and project management

The impact of the ideas related to complexity on management, project management and studies of sustainability at the macro- and micro-levels is self-evident. In case of the terms "complex" and "complexity", contrary to the studies of agile and agility, where the problems deriving from polysemy and semantic diffusion are caused by excessively broad and fuzzy interpretations, the situation is somehow different. The number and variety of interpretations are also large but they can be identified, separated and ordered more precisely, e.g., mathematical models labelled as complexity science developed under the auspices of the Santa Fe Institute (Mitchell 2009) and, on the other side, qualitative interpretations of the complexity of social systems proposed by Luhmann (2013), Stacey *et al.* (2000) or Snowden and Goh (2021). The scheme elaborated by Castellani and Gerrits (2021) illustrates a possibility of at least a partial ordering of complexity-related ideas.

Although the complexity-related ideas also influence the studies of sustainability at all scales, our study is focused on their uses in all areas of project management. A closer look at the applications of the ideas related to complexity in management and project management leads to the conclusion that these applications are very similar. That is why a survey of interpretations of complexity-related ideas in project management can be treated as relevant to the studies of sustainability.

Complexity and complex have become one of the most frequently used terms in modern management and, subsequently, in project management. The scope and difficulties associated with the applications of complexity-related ideas in project management are described in Mesjasz *et al.* (2022). Here only some essential issues are recalled.

There were multiple attempts to develop and to systematize definitions and interpretations of complexity and its related terms. Of 45 interpretations of complexity by Lloyd (2001) and comprehensive synthetizing works, here only some of them are quoted (Gleick 2011; *Encyclopedia of complexity and systems science* 2009; Castellani and Gerrits 2021).

Similarly, from a large number of studies on the role of complexity in project management only selected works are recalled, namely Baccarini (1996), Cicmil *et al.* (2009), Ahern *et al.* (2014), Ireland and Statsenko (2020) and Mikkelsen (2020). It is also worthwhile to recall several influential monographs, e.g., by Williams (2002), Kerzner (2017) and Wysocki (2019).

Referring to the extended typology of applications of complexity-related ideas in project management (Mesjasz *et al.* 2022), in a synthetic approach, the following interpretations of complexity can be enumerated:

- Intuitive complexity embodying hard and soft interpretations of complexity
- Interpretations associated with complexity science: chaos theory and non-linearity, nonequilibrium thermodynamics, complex adaptive systems, cellular automata, edge of chaos, scale-free networks, synergetics of Hermann Haken, catastrophe theory, social systems of Niklas Luhmann

The following distinctive features of intuitive interpretations of complexity (quantitative "hard", qualitative "soft", and the mixed interpretations) can be identified (Mesjasz *et al.* 2022):

- The depiction of complexity often encompasses universal traits that are typically perceived as instinctive, such as the quantity of components, the distinction between these components and their various states, the number and nature of internal interactions, the internal organization of the system (including functional, structural, and power hierarchies, as well as containment hierarchies, indicating structural complexity), and the attributes of interactions between the system (or collective entity) and its surroundings
- The behavior of a system is illustrated through straightforward, intuitive measures both in terms of quantity and quality. For example, this includes the pace of change in elements, their internal interactions, and the overall collective entity, as well as factors like growth, decay, and dissipation..
- Connecting complexity with a lack of adequate measurable data and challenges in acquiring such information .
- The use of the term complexity without any reference object (stand-alone) or in a sense which cannot be sufficiently precisely defined, e.g., complex thinking, complex development, complex behaviour, etc.
- Considering the understanding of complexity as a starting point for various approaches to operationalization, such as system dynamics, system analysis, and system engineering. Viewing complexity as a quantifiable concept, with the assumption that multiple types of complexity exist, thereby justifying the use of the plural term "complexities..

Some additional comments should be added as to understand the various interpretations of complexity in project management. The main sources of complexity-related ideas are associated with broadly defined complexity science described above. All ideas related to complexity in a general sense, and complexity science in particular, are used as mathematical models, analogies and metaphors. It leads to a very cautious approach especially when analogies and metaphors are taken into account. In such case it is absolutely necessary to take into account a necessary level of knowledge of two basic elements of metaphors – the source domain (field) and the target domain (field).

The following types of metaphors are taken into account in the studies of relations between complexity-related ideas and management, including project management: conceptual metaphors, deliberate metaphors, live metaphors and dead metaphors. Lakoff and Johnson (1980) have introduced the conceptual metaphor in which knowledge about the source domain allows for understanding the target domain. According to Steen (2017, pp. 1–2), deliberate metaphor derives from its intentional use between sender and addressee.

In the simplest sense, "live" metaphor reflects a property of an object which is new for it and allows for discovering its new features for example the concept of Morgan (2006) – organization as machine, organization as a living system, etc. "Dead" metaphors on the other hand have evolved further into a situation where the metaphorical meaning has become the meaning for a word or an alternative meaning for a word (polysemy) (Lakoff and Johnson 1980/1995; Cornelissen *et al.* 2008).

In the case of complexity-related ideas two additional aspects have to be added. In addition to their performative character – describing an object as complex – they may have another persuasive value because they are treated as scientific, especially when supported by mathematical models. Therefore, in addition to their performative character, the complexity-related terms can sometimes be treated as persuasive utterances (Sopory and Dillard 2002).

Sustainability: An introductory terminological survey

When considering the interpretations of the terms sustainable, sustainability and sustainable development, it can be concluded that the linguistic barriers in their interpretations are also specific. Sustainability is a typical polysemous notion with fuzzily defined meanings, but contrary to agility and complexity, it is also affected by two challenges: difference of scales in physical and institutional terms and normative character. Agile is already commonly accepted at various but limited and definable scale of organizations and projects. Complexity in management and complexity in project management can be easily distinguished from complexity at other levels – national, regional, global. However, due to the scaling problems and normativity, it is not simple to identify the relations between the meaning of sustainable, sustainability and sustainable development at the global level and in multiple domains at various scales – environmental, economic and social.

The difficulties in defining sustainability and related terms are only briefly discussed as signalize that in studying the relations between project management and sustainability, it is necessary to remember about a more profound and broader context of interpretations.

The idea of sustainability at the global scale was originated in the report *Our common future* prepared under the supervision of Gro Harlem Brundtland. In the report, sustainable development was defined as the development that meets the needs of the current generation, without compromising the needs of future generations (Brundtland 1987, p. 37). The problems with defining sustainability and related ideas were already presented in a report of the International Union of Conservation of Nature (IUCN), the United Nations Environment Programme (UNEP) and World Wide Fund for Nature (WWF) (IUCN/UNEP/WWF 1991, p. 10).Sustainable development, sustainable growth, and sustainable use have been used interchangeably, as if their meanings were the same. They are not. Sustainable growth is a contradiction in terms: nothing physical can grow indefinitely. "Sustainable use" is applicable only to renewable resources: it means using them at rates within their capacity for renewal. "Sustainable development" is used in this context to mean: improving the quality of human life while living within the carrying capacity of supporting ecosystems. A "sustainable economy" is the product of sustainable development. It maintains its natural resource base. It can continue to develop by adapting, and through improvements in knowledge, organization, technical efficiency and wisdom. The idea of three "pillars" of sustainability – social, economic and environmental – proposed by Elkington (1997) has become the core of sustainability discourse at all societal levels (Mesjasz 2016; Purvis *et al. 2019*).

The lack of clarity of interpretations of sustainability is discussed from two basic perspectives. According to the first one, pronounced by Biggiero (2018), the lack of precision of interpretations of sustainability is a consequence of an early development of the sustainability science. The second approach, exposing terminological and linguistic problems of the polysemous, broadly and fuzzily interpretations of sustainability, has been discussed, among others, by Lutz Newton and Freyfogle (2005), Yolles and Fink (2014) and Purvis *et al.* (2019). After a deep linguistic analysis reaching Wittgenstein, Ramsey (2015) observed that due to its broad and normative sense, there is no need to strive for more precise definitions of sustainability. In our considerations we agree with the second approach but at the same time we try to prove that it is necessary to put at least an initial ordering in the discourse on sustainability in management and project management.

According to Lutz Newton and Freyfolgle (2005), when studying the meaning of sustainability from an environmentalist point of view, several paradoxes and doubts have to be considered. A preliminary etymological analysis shows that sustainability is an adjective treated as noun. It derives from an English verb to sustain, that in turn has its roots in the French verb *soutenir*. Both in English and in French these verbs mean to support from below, self-support or to support another actor in their activities or existence (Lutz Newton and Freyfogle 2005, p. 24; *Larousse*, www.larousse.fr/dictionnaires/francais/soutenir/73974). The doubts concern the subjects who are responsible for sustainability – the humans or the nature? Additionally, sustainability is used interchangeably as the goal and a means to achieve the goal, whatever the goal could be. Means are sustainable, if they are repeated over and over. When sustainability is treated as the goal then a question arises what is to be sustained? (Lutz Newton 2005, p. 25). It can be only added that the idea of transition to sustainability as the process leading to the goal that cannot be defined unequivocally can be treated as a method of partially solving this logical dilemma (Loorbach and Rotmans 2010).

A survey of sustainability-related ideas at all scales was developed by Yolles and Fink (2014, pp. 4–5). They argue that there are two main opposing schools of thought in the sustainability-related discourse: the pessimists (called the ecocentrics), consisting generally of groups of ecologists and related others (e.g., nongovernmental organizations, social anarchist politicians), who see that the earth cannot forever support the world's demand of renewable and nonrenewable resources. Second, the optimists (called the egocentrics),consisting generally of groups of economists and related others (e.g., conservative and individualist politicians), who are equally convinced that market incentives, public policies, material substitution, recycling and new technology can together satisfy the needs and improve the quality of human welfare for the future.

As the link between universal meaning of sustainability in management, relevant to projects and project management, Silvius *et al.* (2016, pp. 17–18) formulated six principles of sustainability:

1 Sustainability is about balancing or harmonizing social, environmental and economic interests.
2 Sustainability is about both short- and long-term orientation.
3 Sustainability is about local and global orientation.
4 Sustainability is about consuming income, not capital.
5 Sustainability is about transparency and accountability.
6 Sustainability is about personal values and ethics

As a summary showing the conceptual scope and intricacy of the discussions on sustainability and sustainable development, only two comprehensive examples can be recalled: the Wikipedia Index of sustainability-related articles (https://en.m.wikipedia.org/wiki/Index_of_sustainability_articles) and the UNESCO Sustainable Development website (www.unesco.org/en/sustainable-development).

Sustainability and project management: Patterns of relations

When seen from a linguistic perspective, sustainability is definitely the most polysemous when compared with agile, agility and complexity. Therefore in this part only these characteristics of sustainability are presented that could be helpful in ordering practice and theory associated with agility, complexity and sustainability in project management.

Sustainability and management

Multiple and broad interpretations of the ideas of sustainable, sustainability and sustainable development at the global scale have contributed to the challenges in their transfer to management and project management. Because of the relations between project management and management, an introductory explanations of the role of those three ideas at the corporate level has to be briefly depicted. Additionally, the relation between sustainability-related ideas and corporate social responsibility in business is examined.

Sustainability-related issues are described at the corporate level with the terms corporate sustainability, business sustainability, sustainable organizational management and sustainable development. Similarly as in other areas of sustainability-oriented theory and practice the interpretations of these terms are similar or overlapping.

Several attempts were made to identify the challenges of sustainability in business management after the declaration of its universal importance at a global level. A universal background for corporate sustainability – social, environmental (ecological), economic (financial), called sometimes as three pillars or triple bottom line (TBL or 3BL), as well as three P's (people, planet, profit) – was proposed by Elkington (1997).

Sustainability-oriented management theory and practice are facing the following challenges:

- Universal consequences of polysemous meaning of sustainability
- Identification of relations between sustainability in the universal sense (global level) and sustainability in management
- The scope of meaning of sustainability in management
- Consequences of scaling for sustainability in management
- Consequences of various types of companies for sustainability-oriented management

Taking the ideas of Stead and Stead (2017) as a synthesis representing a vast literature, it can be stated that according to the TBL of Elkington (1997), sustainability embodies all areas of company's activity – economic success, environmental protection and social responsibility. At the same time, it is a result and an element of coevolution of company and its environment and the foundation of its strategy.

In practice and in theory of management such a broad approach, including all areas of company's activity, although acceptable as a general framework, raises the doubts concerning its logical coherence and applicability. While the economic and environmental aspects of sustainability are undisputable, the meaning of social aspects of a broadly interpreted sustainability seems to be less precise. Subsequently, its inclusion makes an impression that sustainability is just another desire for a universal good and not a source of real improvement of social aspects of corporate activities.

While the role of social attributes of business activities considered under the name of Corporate Social Responsibility (CSR) constitutes an important area of modern management, their relations with corporate sustainability are not to clear. It is even postulated not to relate CSR to sustainability-oriented management. The reasons for this measure were explained by Bansal and DesJardine (2014). In the economic sense, sustainable business management requires temporal trade-offs. Firms must choose between investing less for smaller profits sooner and investing more for greater profits later. CSR does not require trade-offs. It is built on strong ethical assumptions and it must be implemented continuously. Concentration on current interests of stakeholders can undermine the possibility to achieve the future goals. Such a short-term approach desired in some sense in the CSR stands in opposition to the strategic meaning of sustainable management. Obviously social aspects of corporate activity may not be separated from sustainability demanded in management but this divide also has to be taken into account.

Sustainability, projects and project management

The sustainability-related ideas were implemented in practice and theory of project management later than in management. It was underscored in the works published in the first and second decades of the 20th century (Silvius and Schipper 2014; Silvius *et al.* 2016). One of the reasons of such a situation is that epistemological and methodological obstacles associated with the relations between sustainability and project management are even more intricate. In addition to the abovementioned limitations of sustainability management in general sense, the reasons for such a situation are as follows:

- A broad variety and scale of projects leading to the problems with interpretations (from small-scale software development project to large-scale infrastructural projects).
- Time-boundedness and various periodization of project management process; usually when seen from a universal point of view it concerns the distinction of the realization phase, the exploitation phase and the closing phase.
- Inherent complexity of projects resulting from their variety and time-boundedness.
- Different understanding and impact of sustainability at each stage of project management process.

An important terminological issue has to be recalled before further discussion. The dominating terminological idea is project management, but in a more fine-tuned considerations on sustainability and project management, the sustainability-related characteristics of projects must also be borne in mind. In our study only selected consequences of the polysemous character of sustainability in project management and in projects are presented which can be helpful in the ordering of our research area. They were described in the conceptual works (Morfaw 2014; Silvius *et al.* 2016) as well as in several surveys (Silvius and Schipper 2014; Aarseth *et al.* 2017; Chawla *et al.* 2018; Armenia *et al.* 2019).

Interpretations of sustainability in project management can be divided into three groups. The first group embodies attempts to develop comprehensive classical definitions (*definiendum-definiens*). Two examples can be recalled. The first, synthetic one: "Sustainability in the project profession is an approach to business that balances the environmental, social, economic aspects of project-based working to meet the current needs of stakeholders without compromising or overburdening future generations" (Association for Project Management 2019). The second, proposed by Silvius *et al.* (2016, p. 40): "Sustainability in projects and project management is the development, delivery and management of project-organized change in policies, processes, resources, assets or organizations, with consideration of the six principles of sustainability, in the project, its results and its effects".

The second group includes the definitions/interpretations based on enumerations of characteristics of relations between project management and sustainability. As the first example the comprehensive description of fundamentals of project sustainability proposed by Morfaw (2014) is recalled. This interpretation embodies practically all characteristics of projects, e.g., dimensions of project sustainability, elements of sustainable development, examples of sustainable business, characteristics of project sustainability, measurement of project sustainability, project sustainability management. In a similar attempt, Chawla *et al.* (2018, p. 164) identified critical parameters to gauge sustainability in the projects: profitability, safety, transparency, ethicality, nature-friendly, social acceptability, fulfilling stakeholders' and the customer's expectations. Similarly, as in the above case, this interpretation also encapsulates.

The third, holistic approach to practice and theory of sustainability in project management is presented by the leading authors in that field (Silvius *et al.* 2016). Taking the universal interpretations of sustainability and characteristics of relations between management and sustainability as the point of departure, they have developed a logically coherent concept showing the relations of sustainability with project management. This work can be treated as an example of research in which the polysemous character of sustainability is treated in a more rigorous manner.

Treating the abovementioned sources as inspiration, the following issues have been selected as the foreground of the analysis of agility, complexity and sustainability in projects and project management:

- Introducing business agility in a checklist for integrating sustainability in projects and project management.
- Project management treated as the management of project-organized change in organizations, policies, products, services, processes, assets and/or resources, in or between organizations.
- System boundaries of considering sustainability in project management.
- Six principles of sustainability.
- Projects as complex systems and complex project management.
- Integration of sustainability in project management treated as a paradigm shift: from an approach to project management that can be characterized by predictability and controllability of both process and deliverables and is focused on eliminating risks, to an approach that is characterized by flexibility, complexity and opportunity (Silvius *et al.* 2016, p. 88).
- Agile and agility as universal characteristics of projects and project management.

- Inspiration from the Agile methodological frameworks in software development in all types of project management.
- Project management process as a foundation of the studies of the role of sustainability.
- The role of *ISO 26000 Guidance on social responsibility* in theory and practice of project management.

Comprehensive approach to agile, complexity and sustainability in project management

The need to understand contemporary project management better leads to the situation where linking all attributes of agile and agility with complexity and sustainability seems necessary and unavoidable. Comprehensive parallel applications of all these ideas have not been developed yet. Some initial elements of such universal approaches can be found in specialized applications and publications, e.g., Dong *et al.* (2021). There are also direct and indirect references to the Agile methodological frameworks and complexity in the study of sustainability in projects and project management (Silvius *et al.* 2016).

This study can be treated as the source of the following concepts illustrating the relations between sustainability, projects and project management: interpretations of sustainability, principles of sustainability, expected effect of sustainability principles on project management processes.

Three proposals of ordering of research on simultaneous applications of agile/agility, complexity and sustainability in projects and project management are presented. Depending on circumstances, they can be implemented consecutively, separately and parallelly.

1 Size of projects as the foundation of structuring research on agile and agility, complexity and sustainability in projects and project management.
2 Identification of universal cognitive and action-oriented characteristics of the terms agile and agility, complexity and sustainability in projects and project management.
3 The project management process as the framework of ordering of applications of agile and agility, complexity and sustainability.

Agile, complexity and sustainability and the size of projects

While the relations between agile and agility, complexity and projects, and project management can be identified relatively easily, broadly defined sustainability in projects and project management is not always clearly and unequivocally identifiable. It can be observed that the interpretation of sustainability is strongly dependent on physical size of projects such as the territory, number of people participating, engaged technical resources, costs, scope on the Internet.

Therefore the identification of relations between the size of projects and interpretations of sustainability is proposed as the first method of ordering of research

Table 1.1 Universal characteristics of scales of projects

Scale of projects	*Characteristics*
Large scale	Large-scale infrastructure projects; large-scale environment protection projects; construction projects; industrial projects (plants); large-scale technical objects, e.g., ships, aircraft
Medium scale	Medium-scale infrastructure projects; construction projects; industrial projects (plants), medium-scale technical objects – ships, aircraft; information and promotion campaigns; large-scale artistic events, large-scale IT projects and systems, e.g., development of software for large public and private institutions, development of companies operating online, e.g., global search engines, social media; equipment of IT companies (computer centers and networks)
Small scale	Small-scale construction projects, small-scale industrial projects (plants), small-scale technical tools – machinery, ships, aircraft; information and promotion campaigns; medium-scale artistic events; medium- and small-scale IT projects and systems, e.g., development of software for medium-size organizations, development of companies operating online, e.g., local networks, medium-size enterprises of all kinds
Microprojects	Small construction and engineering projects with limited direct impact on environment; small IT projects with potential indirect impact on sustainability at various scales; small-size enterprises of all kinds

Source: Authors' own research.

Table 1.2 Relations between scale of projects and interpretations of sustainability

Sustainability area / *Scale of project*	*Economic*	*Environmental*	*Social*
Large scale	strong, direct and indirect	strong, direct and indirect	strong, direct and indirect
Medium scale	strong or medium direct and indirect	strong or medium direct and indirect	strong or medium direct and indirect
Small scale	medium weak indirect	medium weak direct and indirect	weak indirect
Microprojects	weak indirect	weak indirect	weak indirect

Source: Authors' own research.

on Agile, complexity and sustainability in projects. A preliminary typology of the size and characteristics of projects is presented in Table 1.1.

Taking into account the relations of the scale of project with broadly defined sustainability, the typology of their mutual relations is proposed in Table 1.2.

The content of Table 1.2 demands an additional explanation. In the preliminary research on relations between agile and agility, complexity and sustainability, the information contained in Table 1.2 allows to develop the following procedure:

1 Identification of degree of complexity of projects (complex, complicated).
2 Identification of agility of projects (agility in a universal sense and relevance of Agile methodological framework).
3 Determining what interpretations of sustainability are most relevant to the projects.
4 Identification of the role of sustainability in management associated with the projects.

Cognitive and action-oriented characteristics

The second ordering of research on the relations of agile and agility, complexity and sustainability with projects and project management includes normative, deliberate, persuasive and performative interpretations of these terms. It is also relevant to management in a universal meaning. Obviously, this ordering is to some extent arbitrary but it allows for a preliminary systematization of the meaning of agile and agility, complexity and sustainability in projects and project management (Table 1.3).

The results presented in Table 1.3 demand for a brief additional explanation concerning agile and agility, complexity and sustainability. Agile and agility in projects and project management possess a strong normative meaning. The short explanation of this situation, based on our earlier discussion, is stemming from the dominance of agile and agility as the patterns of adaptation to the turbulent environment and the need for learning flexibility and adaptation of projects and project management. Interpretation of agile and agility as moderately deliberate utterances means that the aim of achieving higher levels of agility can be defined only in general terms. High persuasive meaning of agile and agility derives directly from their strong normative sense and validity in projects and project management. Weak performativity of the terms agile and agility results from the very strong impact of emergence and self-organization.

Without delving into the interpretations of complexity in project management (Mesjasz *et al.* 2022), it can be observed that complexity concerns projects, their environment and project teams. It has a weak normative negative interpretation sense since in most universal sense, it results from the inherent limitations of

Table 1.3 Characteristics of Agile, complexity and sustainability in projects and project management

Term / *Interpretation*	*Agile/agility*	*Complexity*	*Sustainability*
Normative	highly positive	weakly negative	highly positive
Deliberate	medium	medium	high
Persuasive	high	medium	high
Performative	weak	weak	medium

Source: Authors' own research.

human cognitive capabilities which are unavoidable. Deliberate and persuasive interpretations of complexity in projects and project management are moderate due to the natural sense of complexity. However, although complexity is inherent in social systems, it is difficult to say that it can be created; thus, its performative sense is weak.

Seen from this perspective, it is easy to conclude that sustainability in its interpretations at all societal scale is always highly positive. However, it is somehow natural that it cannot be created solely by declarations.

Project management process as the framework of ordering

The third component of ordering research on agile and agility, complexity and sustainability in project management is built upon the stages of management process identified by Silvius *et al.* (2016). This pattern of ordering research on the role of agile and agility, complexity and sustainability in project management process is described in Table 1.4.

Table 1.4 includes the final pattern of ordering development of projects in which agile and agility, complexity and sustainability must be taken into account. Its implementation is preceded by the ideas and methods presented in Tables 1.1, 1.2 and 1.3. Table 1.4 reflects two foundations of ordering of realization of projects in which sustainability and complexity should be dealt with agile methodological frameworks. Agility of projects should be left for separate considerations.

First, it must be always taken into account that the needs to meet sustainability-related demands is one of the sources of complexity of the projects and project management process. Therefore sustainability-related problems must be considered as an initial step in ordering the project development process.

Second, as a consequence of complexity of the project and the project management process enhanced by inclusion of sustainability-related problems, applications of agile and agility-related conceptual ideas and methodological frameworks are in some sense natural.

Third, in selecting the agile methodological frameworks the following approaches are proposed:

- Application of precisely defined agile methodological framework
- Application of broadly defined agile methodological framework, sometimes composed of mixed existing methodological frameworks
- Elaboration of an indigenous agile methodological framework relevant to the demands deriving from the need to consider sustainability in the project management process and complexity of the project.

The above considerations allow for drawing the following conclusions concerning the role of joint applications of ideas of complexity, agile and sustainability in project management.

First, it can be observed that project management is the first area of social theory and practice where a new specific phenomenon can be observed. Several utterances

Table 1.4 Identification of the role of agile, complexity and sustainability in the project management process

Stages / *Attributes*	*Sustainability*	*Complexity*	*Agile*
Project initiating	Initial identification of sustainability-related factors in the project management process	Initial identification of complexity of the project and its environment deriving from all attributes with a special attention paid to sustainability-related issues	Initial assessment of relevance of agile methodological frameworks Analysis of relevance of components of agile frameworks in the project management
Project planning	Identification of sustainability-related issues in the project management process Planning activities necessary of coping with sustainability-related issues in three areas (economic, environmental, social) in the project management process Elaboration of criteria necessary for maintaining maximally achievable level of relevance to the demands deriving from sustainability Exposing the dominant role of sustainability-related issues in the process of project management Initial identification of sustainability-related issues in the project	Identification of complexity (environment and project) Preparations of methodological approaches of dealing with complexity Preliminary preparations of the project teams designated to deal with complexity of project and its universally defined environment complexity Exposition of sustainability-related determinants of project management complexity and project complexity	Identification of criteria of selection of an agile methodological framework relevant to demands created by complexity of the process of project management and of the project Selection of a specific precisely defined relevant framework from the collection of agile concepts Attempts to develop sufficiently precisely defined indigenous agile methodological framework

Project executing	Applying relevant selected agile methodological frameworks allowing to deal with complexity and sustainability in the project management process Inclusion the sustainability-related characteristics of the project in the project execution	Creating awareness of complexity in the project team Complete identification of complexity (environment and project) Managing complexity of project by the project team Managing complexity of activities of the project team (self-organization, self-management)	Application of a specific framework from the collection of agile concepts Application of precisely defined elements drawn from various agile methodological frameworks Application of sufficiently precisely defined indigenous agile methodological framework
Project monitoring and controlling	Continuous assessment of relevance of the execution of the project with sustainability-related demands	Continuous assessment of managing complexity of the project and complexity of activities of the project team	Monitoring relevance and effectiveness of the selected agile methodological ramework Constant adaptation of the selected agile-related methodological framework in the process of execution
Project closing	Summary and publication of sustainability-related results in the project management process and in the project	Description of results of dealing with complexity caused and sustainability-related factors and other determinants	Identification of relevance/necessity of applications of agile methodological framework, or its element in closing the project

Source: Authors' own research.

with a polysemous meaning – complexity, agile and agility, and sustainability – are applied to describe and to analyze the projects, the processes of their preparations and the project management teams.

References

Aarseth, W., Ahola, T., Aaltonen, K., Økland, A. and Andersen, B. (2017) Project sustainability strategies: A systematic literature review, *International Journal of Project Management*, Vol. 35, No. 6, pp. 1071–1083. https://doi.org/10.1016/j.ijproman.2016.11.006

Abrahamsson, P., Oza, N. and Siponen, M. T. (2010) Agile software development methods: A comparative review, in: T. Dingsøyr, T. Dybå and N. B. Moe (eds.), *Agile software development*. Berlin, Heidelberg: Springer-Verlag, pp. 31–59.

Agile practice guide (2017). Newtown Square, PA: Project Management Institute.

Ahern, T., Leavy, B. and Byrne, P. J. (2014) Complex project management as complex problem solving: A distributed knowledge management perspective. *International Journal of Project Management*, Vol. 32, No. 8, pp. 1371–1381. doi: 10.1016/j.ijproman.2013.06.007

Aoyama, M. (1998) Web-based Agile software development. *IEEE Software*, Vol. 15, No. 6, pp. 56–65.

Armenia, S., Dangelico, R. M., Nonino, F. and Pompei, A. (2019) Sustainable project management: A conceptualization-oriented review and a framework proposal for future studies. *Sustainability*, Vol. 11, No. 9, 2664. doi: 10.3390/su11092664

Association for Project Management (APM) (2019) *APM body of knowledge*, 7th edition. www.apm.org.uk/resources/what-is-project-management/what-is-sustainability-in-project-management/

Austin, J. L. (1962) *How to do things with words*. Oxford: Clarendon.

Baccarini, D. (1996) The concept of project complexity – A review. *International Journal of Project Management*, Vol. 14, No. 4, pp. 201–204. doi: 10.1016/0263-7863(95)00093-3

Baker, J. (1996) Agility and flexibility: What's the difference? Cranfield School of Management Working Papers Series, SWP 5/96, pp. 1–7. https://dspace.lib.cranfield.ac.uk/bitstream/handle/1826/1151/SWP05-96.pdf?sequence=1

Bansal, P. and DesJardine, M. R. (2014) Business sustainability: It is about time. *Strategic Organization*, Vol. 12, No. 1, pp. 70–78.

Berger, P. L. and Luckmann, T. (1966) *The social construction of reality: A treatise in the sociology of knowledge*. New York: Penguin Putnam.

Biggiero, L. (2018) Providing sound theoretical roots to sustainability science: Systems science and (second-order) cybernetics. *Sustainability Science*, Vol. 13, pp. 1323–1335. https://doi.org/10.1007/s11625-018-0573-2

Bridgman P. W. (1955) *Reflections of a Physicist*. New York: Philosophical Library.

Brown, J. L. and Agnew, N. McK. (1982) Corporate agility. *Business Horizons*, Vol. 25, No. 2, pp. 29–33.

Brundtland, G. H. (1987) *Our common future: World Commission on Environment and Development*. Oxford: Oxford University Press.

Burrell, G. and Morgan, G. (1979/1998) *Sociological paradigms and organisational analysis: Elements of sociology of corporate life*. Aldershot: Gower.

Castellani, B. and Gerrits, L. (2021) *Map of complexity sciences*. Art & Science Factory. www.art-sciencefactory.com/complexity-mapfeb09.html

Chawla, V. K., Chandab, A. K., Angra, S. and Chawla, G. R. (2018) The sustainable project management: A review and future possibilities. *Journal of Project Management*, Vol. 3, pp. 157–170.

Cicmil, S., Cooke-Davies, T., Crawford, L. and Richardson, K. (2009) *Exploring the complexity of projects: Implications of complexity theory for project management practice*. Newtown Square, PA: PMI (Kindle edition).

Cockburn, A. (2007) *Agile software development. The cooperative game*, 2nd edition. Boston: Pearson Education (Kindle edition).

Conforto, E. C., Salum, F., Amaral, D. C., da Silva, S. L., & de Almeida, L. F. M. (2014) Can agile project management be adopted by industries other than software development? *Project Management Journal*, Vol. 45, No. 3, pp. 21–34. https://doi.org/10.1002/pmj.21410

Cornelissen, J. P., Oswick, C., Christensen, L. T. and Phillips, N. (2008) Metaphor in organizational research: Context, modalities and implications for research. *Organization Science*, Vol. 29, No. 1, pp. 7–22. doi: 10.1177/0170840607086634

Dertouzos, M. L., Lester, R. K. and Solow, R. M. (1989) *Made in America: Regaining the productive edge*. Cambridge, MA: MIT Press.

Dong, H., Dacre, N. and Bailey, A. (2021) Sustainable agile project management in complex agriculture projects: An institutional theory perspective. *Advanced Project Management*, Vol. 21, No. 3, pp. 1–7. Available at SSRN: https://ssrn.com/abstract=3829912 or http://dx.doi.org/10.2139/ssrn.3829912

Dove, R. (1991) *21st century manufacturing enterprise strategy – An industry-led view*. Bethlehem, PA: Iacocca Institute, Lehigh University. www.academia.edu/22216161/21st_Century_Manufacturing_Enterprise_Strategy_an_Industry_led_View

Dove, R. (1999) Knowledge management, response ability, and the agile enterprise. *Journal of Knowledge Management*, Vol. 3, No. 1, pp. 18–35. https://doi.org/10.1108/13673279910259367

Duguay, C. R., Landry, S. and Pasin, F. (1997) From mass production to flexible/agile production. *International Journal of Operations & Production Management*, Vol. 17, No. 12, pp. 1183–1195.

Elkington, J. (1997) *Cannibals with Forks: The triple bottom line of twenty-first century business*. Oxford: Capstone.

Encyclopedia of complexity and systems science (2009). Edited by R. A. Meyers. New York: Springer Science + Business Media.

Gell-Mann, M. (1994) *The quark and the jaguar: Adventures in the simple and the complex*. London: Abacus.

Gleick, J. (2011) *Chaos: Making a new science*. New York: Open Road Media.

Goldman, S. L., Nagel, R. N., and Presiss, K. (1995). *Agile competitors and virtual organizations*. New York: Van Nostrand Reinhold.

Gunasekaran, A. (1998) Agile manufacturing: Enablers and an implementation framework. *International Journal of Production Research*, Vol. 36, No. 5, pp. 1223–1247. https://doi.org/10.1080/002075498193291

Gunasekaran, A. (1999) Agile manufacturing: A framework for research and development. *International Journal of Production Economics*, Vol. 62, No. 1–2, pp. 87–105. https://doi.org/10.1016/S0925-5273(98)00222-9

Highsmith, J. (2002) *Agile software development ecosystems*. Boston, MA: Addison-Wesley.

Highsmith, J. (2010) *Agile project management, Creating innovative products*, 2nd edition. Upper Saddle River, NJ: Addison-Wesley (Kindle edition).

Highsmith, J. and Cockburn, A. (2001) Agile software development: The business of innovation. *Computer*, Vol. 34, No. 9, pp. 120–127. doi: 10.1109/2.947100

Highsmith, J. A. III (2000) *Adaptive software development. A collaborative approach to managing complex systems.* New York: Dorset House (Kindle edition).

Ireland, V. and Statsenko, L. (2020) Managing complex projects and systems: A literature synthesis. *Australian Journal of Multi-Disciplinary Engineering*, Vol. 16, No. 1, pp. 93–110. doi: 10.1080/14488388.2020.1805861

ISO 26000 Guidance on social responsibility. (2021). www.iso.org/files/live/sites/isoorg/files/store/en/PUB100258.pdf

IUCN/UNEP/WWF (1991) *Caring for the earth: A strategy for sustainable living*. Gland, Switzerland.

Kerzner, H. (2017) *Project management: A systems approach to planning, scheduling, and controlling*, 12th edition. Hoboken, NJ: Wiley.

Kettunen, P. (2009) Agile software development in large-scale new product development organization: Team-level perspective, Doctoral Dissertation, Helsinki University of Technology. http://lib.tkk.fi/Diss/2009/isbn9789522481146

Kiklewicz, A. (2006a) Dyfuzja semantyczna w języku i w tekście (I) (Semantic diffusion in language and in text) (part I). *LingVaria*, Vol. 1, pp. 9–22.

Kiklewicz, A. (2006b), Dyfuzja semantyczna w języku i w tekście (II) (Semantic diffusion in language and in text) (part II). *LingVaria*, Vol. 2, pp. 9–22.

Kim Schirrmacher, A. and Schopp, M. (2018) Agility in information systems – A literature review on terms and definitions. *Social Transformation – Proceedings of the 23rd UK Academy for Information Systems Conference*, UKAIS 2018, St. Anne's College, Oxford, UK, March 20–21, 2018. https://aisel.aisnet.org/cgi/viewcontent.cgi?article=1024&context=ukais2018

Lakoff, G. and Johnson, M. (1980/1995) *Metaphors we live by*. Chicago: University of Chicago Press.

Leydesdorff, L. (2011) 'Meaning' as a sociological concept: a review of the modeling, mapping and simulation of the communication of knowledge and meaning. *Information sur les Sciences Sociales*, Vol. 50, No. 3–4, pp. 391–413.

Lloyd, S. (2001) Measures of complexity: A nonexhaustive list. *IEEE Control Systems Magazine*, Vol. 21, No. 4, pp. 7–8. doi: 10.1109/MCS.2001.939938

Loorbach, D. and Rotmans, J. (2010) The practice of transition management: examples and lessons from four distinct cases. *Futures*, Vol. 42, pp. 237–246.

Luhmann, N. (2013) *Introduction to systems theory*. Cambridge: Polity.

Lutz Newton, J. and Freyfogle, E. T. (2005) Sustainability: A dissent. *Conservation Biology*, Vol. 19, No. 1, pp. 23–32. Retrieved 01/11/2013 from http://onlinelibrary.wiley.com/doi/10.1111/j.1523-1739.2005.538_1.x/full

Manifesto for Agile Software Development (2001). http://agilemanifesto.org/

Martin Fowler. (2006). Semantic diffusion. https://martinfowler.com/bliki/SemanticDiffusion.html

Mesjasz, C. (2016). Sustainability and complexity: A few lessons from modern systems thinking, in: H. G. Brauch, Ú. Oswald Spring, J. Grin and J. Scheffran (eds.), *Handbook on sustainability transition and sustainable peace.* Cham: Springer International, pp. 421–450.

Mesjasz, C., Bartusik, K., Małkus, T. and Sołtysik M. (2022) *Agile project management and complexity: A reappraisal.* London and New York: Routledge/Taylor & Francis Group.

Mikkelsen, M. F. (2020) The complex project complexity – Identification of five ideal research types. *Journal of Modern Project Management*, Vol. 7, No. 4. www.journalmodernpm.com/index.php/jmpm/article/view/JMPM02201

Mitchell, M. (2009) *Complexity. A guided tour*. Oxford: Oxford University Press.

Morfaw, J. (2014) Fundamentals of project sustainability. Paper presented at PMI® Global Congress 2014, Phoenix, AZ. Newtown Square, PA: Project Management Institute. www.pmi.org/learning/library/fundamentals-project-sustainability-9369

Morgan, G. (2006). *Images of organization, (latest edition)*. Newbury Park, CA: Sage Publications.

Nagel, R. (1992) *21st century manufacturing. Enterprise strategy*. Lehigh University, Iacocca Institute. www.researchgate.net/publication/235112061_21ST_Century_Manufacturing_Enterprise_Strategy_Report

Ortony, A. (ed.) (1993) *Metaphor and thought*, 2nd edition. Cambridge: Cambridge University Press.

Principles behind the Agile Manifesto (2001). http://agilemanifesto.org/principles.html

Project Management Institute (PMI) (2012) *Organizational agility. PMI's pulse of the profession in-depth report*. www.pmi.org/-/media/pmi/documents/public/pdf/white-papers/org-agility-where-speed-meets-trategy.pdf?rev=a988026ae41c42b1921d2a8abbd0dabf

Purvis, B., Mao, Y. and Robinson, D. (2019) Three pillars of sustainability: in search of conceptual origins. *Sustainability Science*, Vol. 14, pp. 681–695. https://doi.org/10.1007/s11625-018-0627-5

Ramsey, J. L. (2015) On not defining sustainability. *Journal of Agricultural and Environmental Ethics*, Vol. 28, No. 6, pp. 1075–1087. https://doi.org/10.1007/s10806-015-9578-3

Rigby, D. K., Sutherland, J., and Takeuchi, H. (2016) Embracing agile. *Harvard Business Review*, May.

Searle, J. R. (1995) *The construction of social reality*. New York: Free Press.

Silvius, A. J. G. and Schipper, R. (2014) Sustainability in project management: A literature review and impact analysis. *Social Business*, Vol. 4, No. 1, pp. 63–96.

Silvius, G., Schipper, R., Planko, J. van den Brink, J. and Köhler A. (2016) *Sustainability in project management* (Routledge Frontiers in Project Management). London/New York: Routledge (Kindle edition).

Snowden, D. and Goh, Z. (2021) *Cynefin – Weaving sense-making into the fabric of our world*. Singapore: Cognitive Edge Pte (Kindle edition).

Sopory, P. and Dillard, J. P. (2002) The persuasive effects of metaphor: A meta-analysis. *Human Communication Research*, Vol. 28, No. 3, pp. 382–419.

Stacey, R. D., Griffin, D. and Shaw, P. (2000) *Complexity and management. Fad or radical challenge to systems thinking*. London and New York: Routledge.

Stead, J. G. and Stead, W. E. (2017) *Management for a small planet*. London/New York: Routledge (Kindle edition).

Steen, G. (2017) Deliberate metaphor theory: Basic assumptions, main tenets, urgent issues. *Intercultural Pragmatics*, Vol. 14, No. 1, pp. 1–24.

Stevens, S. S. (1968) Measurement, statistics and the schemapiric view. *Science*, Vol. 161, pp. 849–856.

Tan, B. (1998) Agile manufacturing and management of variability. *International Transactions in Operational Research*, Vol. 5, No. 5, pp. 375–388. https://doi.org/10.1111/j.1475-3995.1998.tb00121.x

Tuggy, D. (1993) Ambiguity, polysemy, and vagueness. *Cognitive Linguistics*, Vol. 4, no. 3, pp. 273–290. doi: 10.1515/cogl.1993.4.3.273

Vicente, A. and Falkum, I. L. (2017) Polysemy. *Oxford Research Encyclopedia of Linguistics*. https://oxfordre.com/linguistics/display/10.1093/acrefore/9780199384655.001.0001/acrefore-9780199384655-e-325?print=pdf

Williams, T. (2002) *Modelling complex projects*. Chichester: Wiley.

Wysocki, R. T. (2019) *Effective project management. Traditional, agile, hybrid, extreme*, 8th edition. Indianapolis, IN: Wiley.

Yolles, M. and Fink, G. (2014) The sustainability of sustainability. *Business Systems Review*, Vol. 3, No. 2, pp. 1–32.

2 Integrating sustainability and project success

A stakeholder value approach

Ewa Sońta-Drączkowska

Setting the context

In recent years, the integration of project management and sustainability goals has garnered significant attention in both theory and practice. This growing trend aligns with the increasing emphasis on corporate social responsibility (CSR) and the heightened prioritization of environmental, economic, and social factors on top management agendas. These considerations impact also strategic decisions and selection and implementation of projects. The theoretical landscape has undergone a fundamental shift, moving away from a narrow focus on shareholder interests and value maximization, as proposed by shareholder theory (Friedman, 1962), toward a stakeholder theory perspective that advocates for the recognition of the interests of a diverse range of stakeholders within the firm (Freeman, 1984). This shift is rooted in the normative principles of stakeholder theory, which assert the moral entitlement of all organizational stakeholders (Donaldson & Preston, 1995). Therefore, embracing stakeholders outside the organization and the acknowledgment of their importance in the organizational settings is especially valid in the sustainability context (Derakhshan et al., 2019). From the project management perspective, the focal point of this chapter, it becomes crucial to identify the key stakeholders of both the company and the project, determining whose concerns should be accounted for in project stakeholder management and how to effectively manage projects in alignment with defined sustainability objectives.

Another crucial concept in this context is the notion of project success. When assessing project goals that stem from sustainability, it becomes necessary to define and incorporate specific criteria as an integral part of project success evaluation. However, the concept of project success itself is a broad and multifaceted phenomenon that has been extensively discussed in previous studies on project management (Korhonen et al., 2023). Consequently, evaluating sustainability goals and their impact on project success within the context of multiple stakeholders poses a complex and challenging task. Numerous questions arise: How can these two concepts be comprehended, scoped, and interconnected? How can strategic sustainability goals be embedded and integrated into project management throughout the project lifecycle? What is the current state of knowledge on this topic, and what

DOI: 10.4324/9781003356059-3

potential areas for future research exist? This chapter aims to provide an integrative literature review that addresses these questions.[1]

Stakeholder theory will serve as the underlying theoretical framework for this discussion, given its frequent utilization in scoping sustainability challenges and issues in previous literature (Freeman, 1984; Sánchez, 2015). Moreover, stakeholder management is a distinct knowledge area defined in various project management approaches (Project Management Institute, 2021) and constitutes an integral component of project management (Uribe et al., 2018; Eskerod et al., 2015). The application of stakeholder theory can be extended to project stakeholders, making it an interesting framework for linking sustainability and projects.

Corporate social responsibility, stakeholder theory, and projects

The recognition of corporations' responsibility toward society is not a new concept, and it has gained even more attention in the post-pandemic world and amidst the escalating climate crisis (Latapí et al., 2019). Stakeholder theory acknowledges that organizations have obligations not only to shareholders but also to various interest groups, including customers, employees, suppliers, and the broader community (Asif et al., 2013). This view goes beyond firm's shareholders, and states that whoever is influencing or being influenced by the organization should be considered (Freeman, 1984). Corporate sustainability, which is the capacity of a firm to continue operating over a long period of time, depends on the sustainability of the relationships with their stakeholders (Perrini & Tencati, 2006). The authors contend that developing business-specific indicators requires a systematic approach to stakeholder analysis, wherein organizations engage with stakeholders to identify their key expectations and areas of concern. However, in practice, stakeholder analysis is often conducted in an ad hoc manner (Sánchez, 2015).

From the perspective of prescriptive approaches to project management (Svejvig, 2021), project management methodologies incorporate stakeholder engagement as a distinct knowledge area. This process involves the identification of project stakeholders, planning their engagement, managing stakeholder interactions, and monitoring stakeholder engagement (PMI, 2021). When analyzing projects, stakeholders can generally be categorized into three groups: internal stakeholders directly involved in the project, external stakeholders within the organization but not directly involved in the project, and external stakeholders outside both the project and the organization (Figure 2.1). Different sustainability requirements or goals may apply to specific stakeholder groups. For instance, environmental goals may relate to the product or service, ethical considerations and equitable treatment of employees may address the social aspects of sustainability, while addressing societal needs and demonstrating responsibility toward the planet can encompass a wide range of external stakeholders (e.g., local communities). Consequently, the bundles of goals, project requirements, and project stakeholders can become quite complex, particularly in large projects within a global context.

The project management literature recognizes the significance of project stakeholders in achieving project success for several key reasons. Firstly,

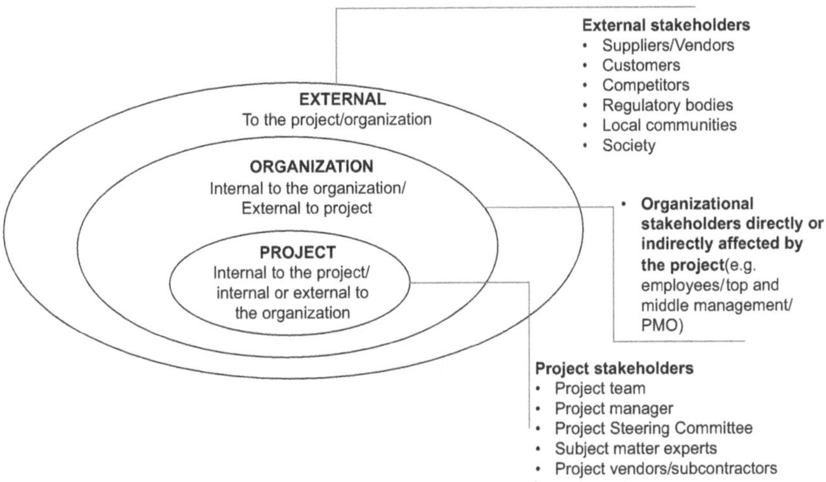

Figure 2.1 Stakeholder groups in the project context.

Source: Own elaboration.

stakeholders play a vital role by providing the necessary contributions, both in terms of financial and nonfinancial resources, to support the project. Secondly, stakeholders often establish the criteria used to evaluate the project's success. Thirdly, the (potential) resistance from stakeholders can introduce various risks and have a detrimental impact on the project's success. Lastly, the project can have both positive and negative effects on stakeholders (Eskerod et al., 2015). Hence, effective stakeholder management entails establishing sustainable project goals that align with stakeholder expectations, as well as the ability to monitor and measure their achievement.

Project stakeholder management is closely tied to the design of project governance. Research indicates that the project's governance structure should incorporate mechanisms to accommodate stakeholder representatives and effectively manage their involvement in decision-making processes, as well as address their concerns and demands (Klakegg et al., 2016). Scholars suggest that governance mechanisms serve several functions, including directing and controlling the organization, balancing various goals (economic, social, environmental, individual), and defining the rights and responsibilities of stakeholders (Müller, 2011). The relationships between organizations and stakeholders are crucial for achieving a delicate balance among economic, social, and environmental dimensions (among others) that underpin sustainability implementation (Uribe et al., 2018). In summary, the combination of CSR strategies, project stakeholder management, and effective project governance forms the foundation for integrating sustainability goals into a company's project management system. Figure 2.2 illustrates the interconnections between the strategic level of an enterprise, portfolio level, and project level. The

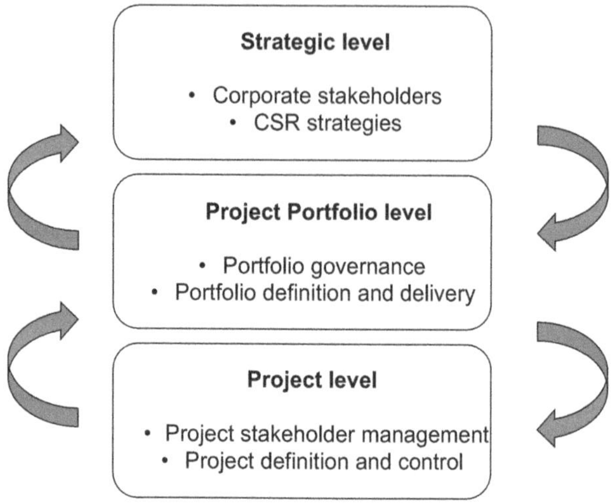

Figure 2.2 Relations between CSR strategies, portfolios, and project.

Source: Own elaboration.

alignment between projects and sustainability goals can occur through both top-down and bottom-up approaches. This is in line with the ways how deliberate and emergent strategies intersect (Kopmann et al., 2017).

Understanding sustainability in projects

The concept of sustainability in projects can be examined from various perspectives (Magano et al., 2021). Current research can be categorized into four major themes:

- Sustainability of the project: This theme addresses the question of whether our project management practices are sustainable. It encompasses the planning, monitoring, and control of project delivery and support processes while considering the environmental, economic, and social aspects of the project's resources, processes, deliverables, and impacts. Key areas include stakeholder identification and engagement, procurement processes, business case development, project monitoring, risk management, and team building.
- Sustainability by the project: This theme explores whether the project's deliverables, outputs, and benefits are sustainable. It focuses on alignment with sustainability goals, innovation, and long-term sustainability. Consideration is given to the environmental, social, and economic impacts of the project's outputs during their specification and design.
- Sustainability of the organization: This theme examines whether the organization as a whole addresses sustainability concerns. It encompasses sustainability

awareness, governance, organizational aspects, and other sustainability considerations that extend beyond individual projects.
- Project managers' ethics and behavior: This theme assesses whether project managers demonstrate ethical and responsible behavior. It emphasizes the social dimension of sustainability and underscores the importance of managerial conduct and work ethics.

Additionally, two cross-cutting dimensions that impact sustainability in projects are:

- Project development life cycle dimension: This dimension focuses on embedding sustainability throughout the entire life cycle of projects. It involves understanding the life cycles involved in a project and their interactions. Practical tools that incorporate sustainability into evaluation processes can facilitate connections between business methodologies and sustainability principles.
- Sustainability-oriented innovations dimension: This dimension examines whether project design and proposed solutions address sustainability issues through innovation. Value innovation that encompasses economic, social, and environmental sustainability dimensions is emphasized, highlighting the need to integrate sustainability concerns into the innovation process.

In summary, there are multiple perspectives through which sustainability in projects can be examined. Sustainable Project Management (SPM) encompasses both the sustainability of project outputs and the integration of sustainability into project management processes across the project life cycle. Research indicates that project managers primarily associate sustainability with the sustainability of the project while sustainability by the project is neglected (Magano et al., 2021).

Furthermore, studies highlight important contingencies in project management when considering the relationship between sustainability and projects: (1) Length of project lifecycle: Sustainability considerations should extend beyond the project life cycle to include the life cycle of project deliverables and final products. However, projects with short life cycles may have limitations in addressing sustainability aspects. (2) Project location: Global competition exposes companies to various global policies, regulations, stakeholders, vendors, and customers. Considering the level of project internationalization (regional, national, or global) becomes crucial in the context of sustainability. (3) Level of uncertainty: Projects inherently involve risks and uncertainties that influence how sustainability is managed. Certain projects, such as large infrastructure projects, may require specific attention to sustainable risk management throughout the project life cycle. (4) Resources usage: Striving to meet infeasible targets in terms of time and efficiency can place excessive pressure on natural, financial, and human resources. This can lead to resource depletion, waste, dissatisfaction, and losses to society and the environment. Taking these contingencies into account is essential for effectively managing sustainability in projects (Chawla et al., 2018).

Linking sustainability to project success

To establish a connection between sustainability and project success, it is essential to first examine the concept of project success. Research confirms that project success is a multidimensional phenomenon, with measures varying depending on factors such as project type, strategic contribution, industry, and stakeholder interpretation (Mir & Pinnington, 2014). The project management literature offers various frameworks for defining project success. The classical metrics used to evaluate project success revolve around the "golden triangle" of scope, time, and cost (Joslin & Müller, 2015). More recent project management standards incorporate additional dimensions of success, such as quality, resources, customer satisfaction, and risk (PMI, 2021). However, these dimensions primarily focus on the efficiency of project management rather than the long-term outcomes or benefits. As the literature has evolved, other dimensions of success have been introduced. Shenhar and Dvir (2007) present a model that evaluates project success across five dimensions: efficiency, impact on customers, impact on the team, business success, and preparation for the future. More recently, the sustainability dimension has been added to this model by Carvalho and Rabechini (2017), encompassing environmental and social perspectives (internal: health and safety; external: external stakeholders and communities). The economic aspect of sustainability was already covered in Shenhar and Dvir's model through the dimensions of success for current and future business. The notion of sustainability is also reflected in the success criteria for international development projects proposed by Ika, Diallo, and Thuillier (2012), including relevance, efficiency, effectiveness, impact, and sustainability.

In the context of new product development projects, one approach to incorporating sustainability measures is by embedding them into the Stage-Gate process as decision criteria (Cooper, 2008). Other authors propose linking sustainability to projects by managing leading variables throughout the project life cycle and assessing sustainability as a lagging success indicator, considering its impact on people, the planet, and financial aspects (Carvalho & Rabechini, 2017). However, some argue that relying solely on performance indicators for monitoring and control may provide an incomplete picture when pursuing sustainability goals. The indicator-centric approach may be problematic as project performance indicators often lag and may not fully capture the value and benefits of a project over its life cycle (Kivilä et al., 2017).

When discussing project success, we can differentiate between the dimension of project enablers, which are factors that facilitate successful project management and drive project outcomes, and the result perspective, which focuses on measuring project outcomes using key performance indicators (Mir & Pinnington, 2014). It is important to consider the assessment timeframe because the project itself can pertain to the project deliverable, which can be verified and assessed immediately upon project closure. Another perspective relates to the expected results or outputs of the project, with the final variable in the chain of project impact being the business benefits that may require post-project evaluation for validation.

Aligned with the latest developments in project management theory, including agile project management, there is a growing emphasis on "customer or user value creation" as a critical parameter of project success. This aligns with agile values, where the customer or user of the product is a key stakeholder and the central focus for assessing the value stream. In this context, the project can be viewed as a "value creation process" aimed at incremental value delivery for the client. This perspective is in line with process-oriented studies in project management (Brunet et al., 2021). Additionally, there are calls to enhance the identification and assessment of strategic non-commercial value in project portfolios, including ecological, societal, and learning values alongside commercial aspects (Martinsuo & Killen, 2014). Table 2.1 provides a summary of the multidimensional perspectives on project management success.

Research suggests that despite the growing interest in linking project management and sustainability, there is still a lack of empirical evaluation concerning the relationship between project sustainability management (PSM) and success (Carvalho & Rabechini Jr., 2017). This may be attributed to the complexity of both

Table 2.1 Multiple dimensions of project success

Measuring dimension	*Various points of reference*	*Implication for sustainability measures*
Project justification/ rationale	• Business case • Customer value delivery • Other type of justification (e.g., public development goals; humanitarian aid; non-commercial value)	What is the project context? What is the project justification? Are sustainability aspects embedded into justification?
Focus of the measurement	• Product of the project (final deliverable) • Process of delivery (project management/ enabling or success factors) • Customer/user value—incremental value delivery • Stakeholder value	Is sustainability a part of our product scope? Is the product sustainable? Is our process of delivery sustainable? Is the customer/user value in line with sustainability? How do we evaluate stakeholder value from projects?
Project parameter/ dimension	• "Golden triangle" measures of project efficiency • Future orientation—creation of the future potentials • Sustainability orientation	Is sustainability embedded into our project evaluation? Does our project meet the criteria that have been setup in the planning?
Outcome perspective	• Deliverable/Product • Result (Output) • Benefit (Outcome) • Value	Do we measure sustainability on the deliverable level, result level, benefit, or value level?

Source: Own elaboration.

project management success and sustainability as phenomena. Moreover, the interpretation of success can vary across business units, project types, industries, and stakeholder groups' understanding of key success indicators. Some authors even argue that measuring a concept as vague as sustainability can be challenging. In fact, taking a purely quantitative approach to sustainability indicators may be counterproductive, as people tend to perceive numbers as absolute truths (Bell & Morse, 2012). Bell and Morse advocate for a holistic qualitative approach when dealing with sustainability indicators. When defining indicators, Levett (1998) highlights that they should be policy relevant, resonant, scientifically valid, and measurable, with the necessary data available. He also notes that the choice of indicators tends to be value-laden and represents the perspective of those responsible for selecting them.

Current research on measuring sustainability in projects is primarily focused on linking the triple bottom line perspective—economic, environmental, and social aspects—to project management performance (Valdes-Vasquez & Klotz, 2013; Madureira et al., 2022). There is a consensus on the three fundamental dimensions of sustainability and their implications for project management, which include a long-term view, consideration of local, regional, and global issues and stakeholders, as well as underlying values. Researchers have introduced a separate "sustainability dimension" to assess project success in terms of sustainability, encompassing the economic, environmental, and social realization and perpetuation of benefits (Martens & Carvalho, 2016).

However, empirical reviews of research results indicate that many initiatives fail to address all three dimensions of sustainability (economic, environmental, and social) and often overlook the trade-offs between these dimensions. Many sustainability initiatives predominantly focus on the environmental dimension while neglecting the social and economic dimensions. This is partly due to the fact that environmental concerns are more heavily regulated, creating pressure to prioritize and meet environmental goals over other dimensions (Madureira et al., 2022).

There are studies that propose even more dimensions of sustainability beyond the triple bottom line (Silvius & Schipper, 2016) and suggest nine dimensions of sustainability along with six project success criteria (Table 2.2). Different

Table 2.2 Framework for linking sustainability and project success

Sustainability is about...	*Project Success*
balancing or harmonizing social, environmental and economic interests both short-term and long-term orientation values and ethics transparency and accountability stakeholder participation risk reduction eliminating waste consuming income, not capital	• The project is executed in a controlled manner • The agreed project deliverable is completed on schedule and within budget • The project deliverable is "fit for purpose" • The business objectives or goals of the project are realized • The stakeholders of the project are satisfied • The project prepares the organization for the future

Source: Silvius and Schipper (2016).

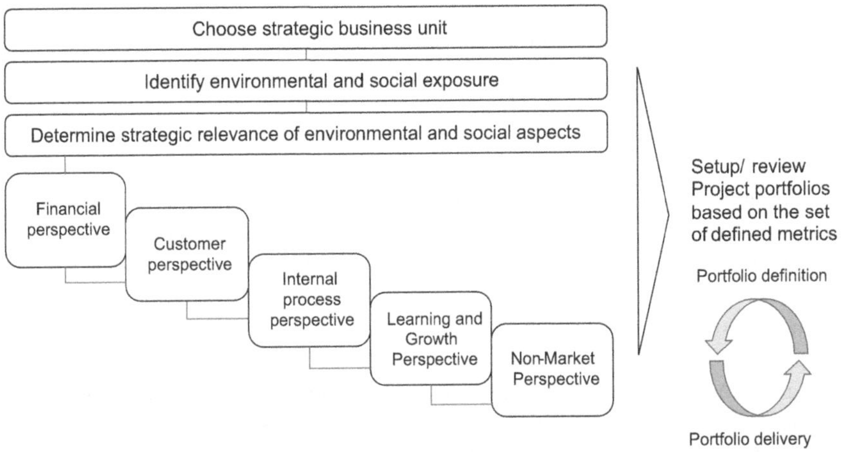

Figure 2.3 Process of formulating a Sustainable Balance Scorecard and link to projects.

Source: Own elaboration based on Figge et al. (2002).

sustainability dimensions may influence the establishment of specific criteria for individual projects.

Strategic view on sustainability in projects

In this section, we propose an approach for interlinking sustainability goals with projects aligned with the organization and its context. One interesting tool for analyzing the alignment between strategic sustainability agendas and projects is the Balanced Scorecard (BSC; Kaplan & Norton, 1992), which has been extended to incorporate the perspective of sustainability (Figge et al., 2002). Initially introduced in the early 1990s as a performance measurement tool for companies with significant intangible assets, the BSC includes financial metrics as outcome measures for overall company success. However, it also incorporates metrics from three additional perspectives: customer, internal processes, and learning and growth, which are seen as drivers for long-term shareholder value creation (Kaplan & Norton, 1992). While the BSC concept initially focused on shareholder value, researchers later expanded the perspective to include other stakeholders and sustainability issues (Figge et al., 2002).

The formulation of the Sustainable Balanced Scorecard (SBSC; Figure 2.3) should meet specific requirements:

- Firstly, the process must lead to an integration of environmental and social management into business management.
- An SBSC that exactly meets the specific characteristics and requirements of the strategy and the environmental and social aspects of a business unit must

not be generic. The process therefore has to ensure, secondly, that the SBSC formulated is business-unit specific.

- Thirdly, environmental and social aspects of a business unit must be integrated according to their strategic relevance. This includes the question whether the introduction of an additional non-market perspective is necessary (Figge et al., 2002).

This approach aligns an organization's strategy with its operational perspective, providing guidance on how to adjust the project portfolio accordingly.

Depending on the strategic business unit selected, various sustainability measures can be justified. The environmental exposure of the business unit needs to be assessed, and researchers propose several dimensions to consider, including emissions (to air, water, soil), waste, material input/material intensity, energy intensity, noise and vibration, waste heat, radiation, and direct intervention on nature and landscape (Figge et al., 2001). Similarly, relevant social aspects can be identified based on the preferences and values of different stakeholders involved (Zadek, 1999, p. 7). A comprehensive framework can be used to systematically identify social issues relevant to a business unit, considering various stakeholder groups (as depicted in Figure 2.1). The next step involves translating the strategic objectives of a business unit into causally linked objectives and indicators. Researchers propose three stages of strategic relevance for environmental and social aspects:

- Environmental or social aspects that represent core strategic issues, requiring the definition of lagging indicators.
- Performance drivers, represented by leading indicators, which demonstrate how the results in each perspective, as reflected by the lagging indicators, can be achieved.
- Hygienic factors, representing environmental or social issues, are also defined as diagnostic indicators. While necessary, they are not sufficient conditions for successfully executing a firm's strategy and thus not included in the BSC (Figge et al., 2002).

Environmental and social aspects should be classified and integrated into the scorecard system based on their strategic relevance, similar to other potentially significant aspects. By following this approach, a system of key performance indicators can be established to support portfolio decisions in project definition, justification, scoping, and delivery.

Agile project management and sustainability

In recent studies, researchers have explored the relationship between agile project management and sustainability (Gomez Silva et al., 2022; Zakrzewska et al., 2022). Agile project management, rooted in software development, formulates a set of values and principles that optimize software engineering. While respecting traditional approaches, agile places greater emphasis on customer collaboration, individual interactions, focusing on the working product, and responding to change (Beck et al., 2001). These practices have since expanded beyond the software industry and are now applied to various types of projects. Large organizations are also experimenting with hybrid approaches, combining traditional and agile methods to implement projects. The major benefits of agile include accelerated time to market, delivery predictability, lower risk, and better adaptability to changes (State of Agile, 2023). Agile methodologies seem well-suited to address sustainability goals. However, the literature presents conflicting observations regarding the benefits of agile in the sustainability context.

On one hand, some argue that agile project management is more sustainable than traditional approaches (Zakrzewska et al., 2022). Agile methodologies prioritize teamwork and stakeholder engagement, which increases the significance of the social aspect, a fundamental pillar of sustainable development. Agile and SPM share common points such as long-term orientation, stakeholder interests, and value orientation (Khizar et al., 2021). There are also attempts to integrate sustainability into the triple bottom line framework (Table 2.3) (Gomez Silva et al., 2022).

On the other hand, there are contributions that discuss the potential side effects of agile approaches, which may hinder the achievement of sustainability goals. The primary advantage of implementing agile is improving time-to-market, a crucial competitive factor (State of Agile, 2023). However, this measure of agile project success may not necessarily align with sustainability goals. The focus on reducing time-to-market often leads to the generation of more products or new versions of products, delivering them quickly, or placing teams under pressure to deliver more within a limited timeframe. For instance, the increasing customer demand for flexibility and rapid delivery in logistics may contribute to additional air pollution. Some critical studies have already highlighted that a strong emphasis on agility may

Table 2.3 Agile project management and sustainability

Social	*Economic*	*Environmental*
• Decision-making • Learning • Meaning making • Self-org • Trust • Collaboration/ Communication • Motivation • Stress reduction • Commitment/ Ownership	• Stakeholder's management • Political and public management • Engagement and innovation • Economic performance • Company–customer relationship management • Value chain • Quality management • Productivity	• Environmental resources • Legislation • Environmental involvement • Certification and environmental education • Sustainable consumption of environmental resources • Environmental policy and management system • Commitment, scope, and dissemination of environmental policies and criteria

Source: Gomez Silva et al. (2022).

inhibit innovation or create significant pressure on teams, potentially leading to burnout (Khanagha et al., 2022). Therefore, studying the impact and prerequisites of agile approaches in the context of achieving sustainable project goals remains an interesting area for research.

Future research areas

Future studies may focus to shed light on achieving sustainability by projects, e.g., how to design projects, products, and services to achieve sustainable goals and what key performance indicators need to be setup. An interesting area of study is social innovation projects and how to measure their results and benefits. Another relatively unexplored area of study is what are the most important project management practices that help to achieve sustainability goals in projects, moreover, how to integrate sustainable thinking and measurement into project management's body of knowledge, e.g., processes: stakeholder management, life cycle management, decision-making, procurement. Furthermore, we need knowledge on how to develop project managers' competencies necessary for managing sustainable projects (Marcelino-Sádaba et al. 2015). Another interesting area of study is studying paradoxical tensions arising when managing sustainable project objectives, e.g., short-term versus long-term perspective on projects outcomes or using economic versus paradoxical decision frame (Sabini & Alderman, 2021). The first decision frame leads the manager to focus only on the environmental and social aspects aligned with economic objectives (i.e., sustainability issues are considered pragmatically in conjunction with positive economic benefits for the organization). The paradoxical frame leads managers to develop a dual interpretation of sustainability issues, accepting the fact that addressing various "desirable but interdependent outcomes simultaneously leads to a risk of unintended consequences" (Sabini & Alderman, 2021). Last but not least, there is still room for research on if and when agile project management is in line with sustainability objectives.

Future studies should aim to shed light on achieving sustainability through projects. For example, research could focus on how to design projects, products, and services that align with sustainable goals and identify key performance indicators that should be established. Another interesting area of study is how to achieve sustainability by projects, e.g., social innovation projects and how to measure their results and benefits. Additionally, there is a relatively unexplored field of research on the most important project management practices that contribute to achieving sustainability goals in projects. Furthermore, understanding how to integrate sustainable thinking and measurement into the project management's body of knowledge is essential, including areas such as stakeholder management, life cycle management, decision-making, and procurement processes. It is also crucial to develop project managers' competencies necessary for managing sustainable projects (Marcelino-Sádaba et al., 2015).

Another interesting area of study is exploring the paradoxical tensions that arise when managing sustainable project objectives. These tensions include balancing short-term and long-term perspectives on project outcomes and navigating economic versus paradoxical decision frames (Sabini & Alderman, 2021). The economic decision frame focuses on aligning environmental and social aspects with economic objectives, pragmatically considering sustainability issues alongside positive economic benefits for the organization. On the other hand, the paradoxical decision frame involves accepting the inherent complexity of sustainability issues and acknowledging that pursuing multiple interdependent outcomes simultaneously may result in unintended consequences. Finally, there is still a need for research to investigate the alignment between agile project management and sustainability objectives. Understanding when and how agile methodologies can effectively contribute to sustainability objectives is an important area to explore.

Note

1 The source of data are journal articles in full version and English, selected from Web of Science based on the combination of the following search criteria "Project Management" and "Sustainability"; "Project Management" and "Sustainability measures"; "Project success" and "Sustainability"; "Project success measures" and "Sustainability".

References

Asif, M., Searcy, C., Zutshi, A., & Fisscher, O. A. (2013). An integrated management systems approach to corporate social responsibility. *Journal of Cleaner Production,* 56, 7–17.

Beck, K., Beedle, M., Van Bennekum, A., Cockburn, A., Cunningham, W., Fowler, M., ... & Thomas, D. (2001). Manifesto for agile software development. . https://agilemanifesto.org/

Bell, S., & Morse, S. (2012). *Sustainability indicators: Measuring the immeasurable?.* Routledge.

Brunet, M., Fachin, F., & Langley, A. (2021). Studying projects processually. *International Journal of Project Management*, 39(8), 834–848.

Carvalho, M. M., & Rabechini Jr, R. (2017). Can project sustainability management impact project success? An empirical study applying a contingent approach. *International Journal of Project Management*, 35(6), 1120–1132.

Chawla, V., Chanda, A., Angra, S., & Chawla, G. (2018). The sustainable project management: A review and future possibilities. *Journal of Project Management*, 3(3), 157–170.

Cooper, R. G. (2008). Perspective: The stage-gate® idea-to-launch process—update, what's new, and nexgen systems. *Journal of Product Innovation Management*, 25(3), 213–232.

Derakhshan, R., Turner, R., & Mancini, M. (2019). Project governance and stakeholders: A literature review. *International Journal of Project Management*, 37(1), 98–116.

Donaldson, T., & Preston, L. E. (1995). The stakeholder theory of the corporation: Concepts, evidence, and implications. *Academy of Management Review*, 20(1), 65–91.

Eskerod, P., Huemann, M., & Savage, G. (2015). Project stakeholder management—Past and present. *Project Management Journal*, 46(6), 6–14.

Figge, F., Hahn T., Schaltegger S., & Wagner, M. (2001). *Sustainability Balanced Scorecard. Wertorientiertes Nachhaltigkeitsmanagement mit der Balanced Scorecard.* Center for Sustainability Management.

Figge, F., Hahn, T., Schaltegger, S., & Wagner, M. (2002). The sustainability balanced scorecard–linking sustainability management to business strategy. *Business Strategy and the Environment*, 11(5), 269–284.

Freeman, R. E. (1984). Strategic management: A stakeholder approach, *Business Ethics Quarterly*, 1, 53–73.
Friedman, M. 1962. *Capitalism and freedom*. University of Chicago Press.
Gomes Silva, F. J., Kirytopoulos, K., Pinto Ferreira, L., Sá, J. C., Santos, G., & Cancela Nogueira, M. C. (2022). The three pillars of sustainability and agile project management: How do they influence each other. *Corporate Social Responsibility and Environmental Management*, 29(5), 1495–1512.
Ika, L. A., Diallo, A., & Thuillier, D. (2012). Critical success factors for World Bank projects: An empirical investigation. *International Journal of Project Management*, 30(1), 105–116.
Joslin, R., & Müller, R. (2015). Relationships between a project management methodology and project success in different project governance contexts. *International Journal of Project Management*, 33(6), 1377–1392.
Kaplan, R., & Norton, D. (1992) The balanced scorecard—Measures that drive performance. *Harvard Business Review*, 79.
Khanagha, S., Volberda, H. W., Alexiou, A., & Annosi, M. C. (2022). Mitigating the dark side of agile teams: Peer pressure, leaders' control, and the innovative output of agile teams. *Journal of Product Innovation Management*, 39(3), 334–350.
Khizar, H. M. U., Iqbal, M. J., & Rasheed, M. I. (2021). Business orientation and sustainable development: A systematic review of sustainability orientation literature and future research avenues. *Sustainable Development*, 29(5), 1001–1017.
Kivilä, J., Martinsuo, M., & Vuorinen, L. (2017). Sustainable project management through project control in infrastructure projects. *International Journal of Project Management*, 35(6), 1167–1183, ISSN 0263-7863, https://doi.org/10.1016/j.ijproman.2017.02.009
Klakegg, O. J., Williams, T., & Asmamaw, S. (2016). Taming the 'trolls': Major public projects in the making. *International Journal of Project Management*, 34(2), 282–296.
Kopmann, J., Kock, A., Killen, C. P., & Gemünden, H. G. (2017). The role of project portfolio management in fostering both deliberate and emergent strategy. *International Journal of Project Management*, 35(4), 557–570.
Korhonen, T., Jääskeläinen, A., Laine, T., & Saukkonen, N. (2023). How performance measurement can support achieving success in project-based operations. *International Journal of Project Management*, 41(1), 102429.
Latapí Agudelo, M. A., Jóhannsdóttir, L., & Davídsdóttir, B. (2019). A literature review of the history and evolution of corporate social responsibility. *International Journal of Corporate Social Responsibility*, 4(1), 1–23.
Levett, R. (1998). Sustainability indicators—integrating quality of life and environmental protection. *Journal of the Royal Statistical Society: Series A (Statistics in Society)*, 161(3), 291–302.
Madureira, R. C., Silva, C. S., Amorim, M., Ferreira Dias, M., Lins, B., & Mello, G. (2022). Think twice to achieve a sustainable project management: From ecological sustainability towards the Sustainable Project Management Cube Model. *Sustainability*, 14(6), 3436.
Magano, J., Silvius, G., Sousa e Silva, C., & Leite, A. (2021), The contribution of project management to a more sustainable society: Exploring the perception of project managers. *Project Leadership and Society*, 2, 100020, ISSN 2666-7215, https://doi.org/10.1016/j.plas.2021.100020
Marcelino-Sádaba, S., González-Jaen, L. F., & Pérez-Ezcurdia, A. (2015). Using project management as a way to sustainability. From a comprehensive review to a framework definition. *Journal of Cleaner Production*, 99, 1–16.

Martens, M. L., & Carvalho, M. M. (2016). Sustainability and success variables in the project management context: an expert panel. *Project Management Journal*, 47(6), 24–43.

Martinsuo, M., & Killen, C. P. (2014). Value management in project portfolios: Identifying and assessing strategic value. *Project Management Journal*, 45(5), 56–70. https://doi.org/10.1002/pmj.21452

Mir, F. A., & Pinnington, A. H. (2014). Exploring the value of project management: linking project management performance and project success. *International Journal of Project Management*, 32(2), 202–217.

Muller, R. (2011). Project governance. *Strategic Direction*, 27(2). https://doi.org/10.4324/9781315245928

Perrini, F., & Tencati, A. (2006). Sustainability and stakeholder management: The need for new corporate performance evaluation and reporting systems. *Business Strategy and the Environment*, 15(5), 296–308.

Project Management Institute (2021) *Project management body of knowledge,* 7th Edition, Project Management Institute.

Sabini, L., & Alderman, N. (2021). The paradoxical profession: Project management and the contradictory nature of sustainable project objectives. *Project Management Journal*, 52(4), 379–393.

Sánchez, M. A. (2015). Integrating sustainability issues into project management. *Journal of Cleaner Production,* 96, 319–330.

Shenhar, A. J., & Dvir, D. (2007). *Reinventing project management: The diamond approach to successful growth and innovation.* Harvard Business Review Press.

Silvius, G., & Schipper, R. (2016). Exploring the relationship between sustainability and project success-conceptual model and expected relationships. *International Journal of Information Systems and Project Management*, 4(3), 5–22.

State of Agile (2023). 16th Edition, digital.ai.

Svejvig, P. (2021). A meta-theoretical framework for theory building in project management. *International Journal of Project Management*, 39(8), 849–872.

Uribe, D. F., Ortiz-Marcos, I., & Uruburu, Á. (2018). What is going on with stakeholder theory in project management literature? A symbiotic relationship for sustainability. *Sustainability*, 10(4), 1300.

Valdes-Vasquez, R., & Klotz, L. E. (2013). Social sustainability considerations during planning and design: Framework of processes for construction projects. *Journal of Construction Engineering and Management*, 139(1), 80–89.

Zadek, S. (1999). Stalking sustainability. *Greener Management International*, 26, 21–31.

Zakrzewska, M., Piwowar-Sulej, K., Jarosz, S., Sagan, A., & Sołtysik, M. (2022). The linkage between Agile project management and sustainable development: A theoretical and empirical view. *Sustainable Development*, 30(5), 855–869.

3 The role of sustainable dynamics in organizational transformation and project success

Szymon Cyfert and Maciej Zastempowski

Justification of the research gap

While research findings point to the importance of using dynamic capabilities (DC) in the processes of shaping competitive advantage (Badrinarayanan *et al.*, 2019; Fabrizio *et al.*, 2022; Ferreira *et al.*, 2021; Ferreira and Coelho, 2020), it can be noted that companies' attempts to match the complexity of the environment (Amui *et al.*, 2017), linked to the integration of economic, social, and environmental achievements into strategies (Dentoni *et al.*, 2016) and the inclusion of environmental sustainability in new product development (Dangelico *et al.*, 2017) are forcing the need to redefine DC assumptions and turn to Sustainable Dynamics Abilities (SDAs, henceforth). In doing so, it is worth noting that SDAs do not negate the assumptions of the DC concept but represent a deepening and continuation of it (Qiu *et al.*, 2020). Research on SDAs shows that it can have beneficial impacts on implementing cooperate social responsibility (CSR) (Wu *et al.*, 2014), ensuring adaptation and resilience (Amui *et al.*, 2017), capitalizing on technological breakthroughs, optimizing resources, and meeting stakeholder expectations (Karman and Savanevičienė, 2021).

Despite the potentially positive impact of SDA, only a few authors have investigated the link between SDA and organizational transformation. Such a state of affairs can be explained by pointing to the lack of a clear definition of the SDA construct, which hinders the implementation of the research process and the early stages of research on SDA, a consequence of the reason for the sparse theoretical basis and the lack of development of a coherent concept. However, viewing SDA through the lens of the potential benefits of using resources and knowledge to renew and develop an organization's green capabilities (Chen and Chang, 2013) suggests that SDA supports organizational transformation activities. Therefore, in this chapter, we have attempted to investigate how SDA interacts with organizational transformation. At the same time, the complexity of the organizational transformation (Lee *et al.*, 2013; Leifer, 1989; McNulty and Ferlie, 2011; Niemi and Pekkola, 2020) leads us to narrow their consideration to two issues: (1) the impact of SDA on environmental orientation, and (2) the impact of SDA on project success. In justifying the choice of variables studied, we would like to note that we are referring to issues at the "input and output" of organizational transformation.

DOI: 10.4324/9781003356059-4

Indeed, environmental orientation can be considered, in relation to SDA, as a factor enabling the realization of organizational transformation while treating SDA as a coherent mechanism combining external sustainable requirements with the redeployment of internal resources and capabilities (Wu *et al.*, 2014) that forces the need to take into account both internal and external environmental orientation. In contrast, the effectiveness of the implementation of project undertakings can be considered both as a result of the correctness of the implementation of organizational transformation and as the mechanism through which organizational transformation is carried out.

In the empirical part, we use the data from a quantitative study conducted between December 2022 and March 2023 on 382 Polish small and medium enterprises (SMEs). For each of the studied constructs, we used validated scales, i.e., in the case of SDAs, the scale proposed by Karman and Savanevičienė (2021), in terms of environmental orientation – the Banerjee (2001) scale, and for assessing the success of projects – the Aga et al. (2016) scale. We used an ordered logistic regression model to analyze the relationship between the constructs.

The study suggests three issues. Firstly, SDAs have a positive impact on the internal environmental orientation of the surveyed SMEs. Secondly, the impact of the SDA on the external environmental orientation of the surveyed SMEs turned out to be ambiguous. Thirdly, SDAs do not affect all aspects of project success.

The concept of Sustainable Dynamics Abilities

Although the DC perspective is considered an extension of the resource-based approach (RBV), it differs in important ways from the RBV orientation. Indeed, while the static resource orientation pushed in RBV assumes that scarce, valuable, and hard-to-mimic resources are a source of competitive advantage for those companies that control them, the DC perspective points to the desirability of configuring and shaping the resource base (Schilke *et al.*, 2018). The DC construct suggests the existence of two key aspects of competitive advantage formation: dynamics, referring to the nature of changes in the environment, and capabilities, indicating coping with change through internal adjustment of the organization (Teece *et al.*, 1997). Similarly, Eisenhardt and Martin point out that competitive advantage in a dynamic business environment, in which change is frequent and non-linear and market players are not always clearly defined, is achievable only when companies develop and apply capabilities faster, smarter, or more randomly than competitors (Eisenhardt and Martin, 2000). According to the basic premise of the DC concept, companies that have the capacity to integrate, build, and reconfigure internal and external resources according to identified opportunities and changes in the environment can build and maintain a strategic position in a rapidly changing environment (Helfat *et al.*, 2007; Teece *et al.*, 1997). On the other hand, Eisenhardt and Martin define DC as organizational and strategic procedures to integrate, reconfigure, acquire, and release resources to match and create market changes (Eisenhardt and Martin, 2000).

Dentoni et al. (2016) points out that DCs are vital in shaping sustainable competitive advantage in the face of rapid technological change and the uncertain nature of future competition and markets. At the same time, they note that addressing sustainability, due to the need to integrate economic, social, and environmental performance and to value the importance of stakeholders, changes the nature of DCs needed by companies, forcing the need to appeal to sustainable dynamic abilities. Discussing the SDA concept, it should be noted that for reasons already pointed out – the lack of a clear definition of the SDA construct and the early stage of SDA research, there is no consistent nomenclature in the literature. At the same time, the terms *sustainable dynamic capabilities, green dynamic capabilities, sustainability-focused dynamic capabilities, dynamic corporate sustainability capabilities, dynamic management capabilities, CSR, or eco-centric dynamic capabilities* are used interchangeably.

Qiu et al. (2020) suggest that green DC can be considered a deepening and continuation of the concept of the DC. Wu's et al. (2014) results show that companies with DC can develop and implement effective CSR strategies and practices. Amui et al. (2017) recognize that the drive to embed sustainability in the concept of DC stems from attempts to match the complexity of the environment. They point to the need to integrate sustainability with strategy and give it the characteristics of dynamism and innovation to become a competitive factor adapted to the adaptation and resilience. Beske (2012) points out that although the concept of DC refers to achieving sustainable competitive advantage, sustainability in this view cannot be confused with the sustainable development. Also, Karman and Savanevičienė (2021), pointing to the need for sustainable business development in the face of technological breakthroughs, resource depletion, and rising stakeholder expectations, postulate the need to rethink the long-term resilience of organizations to enable sustainable competitiveness through DC.

Dangelico et al. (2017) define sustainability-focused DC as the ability to integrate, build, and reconfigure competencies and resources to incorporate environmental sustainability into new product development in response to market changes. Chen and Chang (2013) define the concept of green DC as a company's ability to use existing resources and knowledge to renew and develop green organizational capabilities to respond to a dynamic market. Qiu et al. (2020) point out that green dynamic capability is the high-level ability of companies to achieve sustainable and green development in an ever-changing environment, emphasizing the integration, construction, and reconfiguration of internal and external environmental resources. Wu et al. (2014) view dynamic corporate sustainability capabilities as a multidimensional construct encompassing the ability of companies to meet rapidly changing stakeholder expectations for sustainability by deliberately changing functional capabilities to achieve economic, environmental, and social competencies simultaneously. They point out three important issues for understanding the dynamic management capabilities of CSR. Firstly, the key challenge of CSR is to strike a balance between public good and corporate interest, which requires consideration of both external and internal considerations. Secondly, DC are considered repeatable procedures, which makes it possible, despite the rapidly changing business and social environment, to use the DC of companies to develop stable and identifiable plans for developing and implementing CSR strategies. Thirdly, a certain level of similarity of DC in different companies makes it possible to assume that CSR management can benefit from applying a common set of DC.

Building on the concept proposed by Teece et al. (1997), Oliveira-Dias et al. (2022) propose a model of sustainable DC that includes three types of DC: sensing, seizing, and transforming. Qiu et al. (2020) assume that DC include (1) the ability to integrate internal and external resources, (2) the ability to reconfigure resources, and (3) the ability to gain insight into the environment. Wu et al. (2014) suggest that the DC for corporate sustainability are composed of three distinct but related sub-capabilities: (1) monitoring capability, focusing on external stakeholder requirements; (2) responsible for relevant internal organizational configurations reconfiguration capability, and (3) integrating other capabilities with seizing capability. A similar arrangement of DC to improve sustainable competitiveness is proposed by Karman and Savanevičienė (2021) distinguishing scanning, sensing, and reconfiguring capabilities. A different approach is proposed by Dangelico et al. (2017) showing that the change in ordinary sustainability-oriented capabilities is influenced by sustainability-oriented DC consisting of three underlying processes: (1) external resource integration; (2) internal resource integration; (3) resource building and reconfiguration. Referring to the linkage between the concepts of DC and sustainable supply chain management resulting from the similarity of environmental and organizational conditions, Beske (2012) distinguishes the following DC: knowledge assessment, supply chain partner development, co-evolving reflexive supply chain control, and supply chain re-conceptualization. In subsequent studies, Beske et al. (2014) expand the list of DC to nine variables: (1) knowledge assessment; (2) knowledge acquisition; (3) capability development; (4) search, selection, and integration; (5) supply chain link foundation; (6) product, process development; (7) relationship management; (8) transparency; (9) control and monitoring. Borland et al. (2016) point to the need to expand the boundaries of the DC framework to include the environment, which allows them to distinguish five eco-centric DC: sensing, seizing, reconfiguring, remapping, and reaping.

Environmental orientation and Sustainable Dynamics Abilities

Chavez et al. (2021) define environmental orientation as a bundle of cultural and human resources that generate environmental performance and provide the necessary perspective and driving force to characterize and collate resources as an external environmental information exchange. Chan et al. (2012) emphasize that environmental orientation refers to management's recognition of the importance of environmental issues facing businesses. Chan and Ma (2016) suggest that environmental orientation is manifested by the degree of synthesis of environmental values with corporate culture. Pointing to the common ground between environmental orientation and market orientation, Gabler et al. (2015) point out two features that differentiate the two approaches: (1) knowledge of the environment and its role in the business landscape, (2) a balance of emphasis on primary and secondary stakeholders.

Banerjee (2002) divides environmental orientation into internal and external environmental orientation, assuming that, while internal environmental orientation is a construct similar to a pro-environmental culture, external environmental orientation has similarities with the organizational climate. A similar dichotomous division of environmental orientation is proposed by Saleem et al. (2021) assuming that environmental orientation is an ability based on natural resources resulting from internal or external pressures. Salvador and Burciaga (2020) point out that an organization's internal environmental orientation reflects its commitment to environmental ideals within its "boundaries" and represents the degree to which pro-environmental values are promoted among employees and within the company's operations. In contrast, an organization's external environmental orientation represents the degree to which the company integrates its pro-environmental values into its relationships with external stakeholders. Similar assumptions are made by Zhou et al. (2020) showing that internal environmental orientation reflects a company's internal standards for ethical behavior, commitment, and environmental values, which are embedded in the company's structures and routines, while external environmental orientation is driven by external stakeholders, which requires awareness of and meeting the environmental requirements of stakeholders.

The results of Fraj-Andrés et al. (2009) suggest that an organization's environmental orientation positively affects its commercial performance. Similar insights are derived by Zhou et al. proving that environmental orientation is positively correlated with company performance. Gabler et al. (2015) see the existence of a positive relationship between environmental orientation and the environmental capability. Also, Ozgul's (2022) results indicate that environmental orientation, which is a strategic organizational resource, can significantly support the green absorptive capacity. Zameer et al. (2022) note that environmental orientation emphasizes organizational capability, which is a strategic and active internal capability. Aboelmaged (2018) observes that environmental orientation emphasizes an organizational capability that meets current and future environmental and social needs while meeting the organization's economic goals. Agyabeng-Mensah et al. (2023) suggests that environmental orientation is a capability that plays an important role in sustainability practices to achieve desired outcomes. They emphasize that environmental orientation promotes pro-environmental behavior and encourages the development of environmental strategies to enhance performance. Therefore, we propose the following research question:

> RQ_1: Do sustainable dynamic abilities positively influence SMEs' environmental orientation?

Project success and Sustainable Dynamics Abilities

Although the construct of project success is currently in project management and has been widely studied (Albert *et al.*, 2017; Alvarenga *et al.*, 2019), Aga et al.

(2016) point to a perceived lack of consensus in the discussion regarding project success criteria.

Albert et al. (2017) emphasizing that the basis of almost all approaches to measuring project success is Barnes' Iron Triangle, point out that project success can be understood as both the success of the management of the project and the success of the developed product, which means that the evaluation of the project should consider the aspect of time, costs, and budgets, and should also refer to the achievement of company goals, project objectives, and customer satisfaction with the product. Leading the discussion on the evolution of project success criteria, Müller (2019) assumes that project success criteria should refer to variables such as quality, stakeholder satisfaction, and knowledge management. Bergmann and Karwowski (2019) note that some studies take a traditional approach, assuming that project success is one-dimensional and linked to the budget, time, and quality of execution. At the same time, some researchers view the construct of project success as a complex, multidimensional concept with many more attributes. Aga et al. (2016) note the importance of the criteria of relevance, effectiveness, efficiency, impact, and sustainability. Khan's et al. (2013) critical analysis of project success criteria provided the basis for proposing a model assuming a balance between hard and soft criteria along five dimensions: project effectiveness, organizational benefits, project impact, stakeholder satisfaction, and potential future. Also, Albert et al. (2017) point out the distinction between hard and soft criteria for assessing project success. Pointing to the multidimensionality of project success criteria, Scott-Young and Samson (2008) note the practice of data reduction based on the assumption that success factors improve all outcomes equally, thus masking the possibility of identifying factors that affect different outcomes.

Hermano and Martín-Cruz (2016) recognize that the relationship between top managers and the performance of projects, portfolios, and companies is mediated by building operational and DC. Examining the relationship between project management and project success from the perspective of agency theory and management theory, Müller (2019) indicates that project success correlates with an increase in the parent organization's stakeholder orientation. Results of Hermano et al. (2022) suggest that dynamic project management capabilities do not directly affect company performance but influence it indirectly by increasing company performance in projects, programs, and portfolios. Examining cognitive factors and higher-order procedures at the project level, they show that DC positively relate to the project performance (Pérez Rave *et al.*, 2022). Findings by Ettlie et al. (2023) show that DC are significantly related to the success of an R&D project mediated by a strategic objective. Emiliano de Souza et al. (2022) note that although DC positively influence project success, their impact on dimensions of success varies. Mohd Naim Yassien and Jumaa Alnajjar (2020) point to a significant mediating role of project capabilities between DC and project success. Therefore, we ask a research question:

> RQ_2: Do sustainable dynamic abilities positively influence SMEs' project success?

Materials and methods

Data collection and respondent characteristics

The data was collected using the Computer-Assisted Web Interview (CAWI) from December 2022 to March 2023. The study population was non-financial SMEs in Poland. According to data from the Local Data Bank, in 2020, this population included 63,947 entities (GUS, 2023). The SMEs participating in the survey were randomly selected based on the National Official Register of Business (Statistics Poland, 2023). The minimum sample size was 382 SMEs, assuming a 95% confidence level, 50% fraction share, and a 5% maximum error. The final dataset covered 393 observations. Table 3.1 presents the main characteristics of the respondents.

Construct measurement

Sustainable dynamic abilities (explanatory variables)

We measured the sustainable dynamic abilities based on a 22-statement DC scale developed by Karman and Savanevičienė (2021). This scale measures DC distinguishing three fundamental types: scanning (X_1–X_7), sensing ($X_8 - X_{16}$), and reconfiguring capabilities ($X_{17} - X_{22}$). The respondents answered based on a 5-point Likert scale ranging from 1 – strongly disagree to 5 – strongly agree. To assess the reliability of the measurement, we used Cronbach's alpha, the result of which indicated its internal consistency (0.862). The list of statements and descriptive statistics are presented in Table 3.2.

Environmental orientation (explained variables)

In the case of measuring environmental orientation, we used a scale developed by Banerjee (2001) and used, among others, by Gabler et al. (2015). It is based on assessing environmental orientation in two dimensions: internal ($Y_1 - Y_4$) and external ($Y_5 - Y_7$). Also, here, respondents answered using the 5-point Likert scale. The Cronbach's alpha was 0.837. The list of statements and descriptive statistics are presented in Table 3.3.

Table 3.1 Sample characteristics

Characteristics	*Sample (%)*
Firm size (employees)	
Small – 10–49	73.79
Medium – 50–249	26.21
Activities	
Industry	10.43
Construction	16.03
Trade	21.37
Services	52.17

Table 3.2 Sustainable dynamic capabilities – descriptive statistics

Variable	*Description*	*Median*	*Mode*	*Std. Dev.*	*Variance*
Scanning capabilities					
X_1	Formal and informal communication channels with external stakeholders	4	4	0.727	0.529
X_2	Active dialog with external stakeholders regarding sustainability issue	4	4	0.734	0.539
X_3	Explain organization's strategic sustainability plans and asking for the feedback from external stakeholders	4	4	0.789	0.622
X_4	Steer new sustainable development strategies through public consultation process	4	4	0.979	0.959
X_5	Sense the most relevant and significant environmental issues	4	5	0.931	0.867
X_6	Use the information about the emerging customer preference to guide the development of green market strategy	4	4	0.945	0.894
X_7	Analyze the environment for the development of sustainable innovations	4	5	0.775	0.601
Sensing capabilities					
X_8	Look for new knowledge regarding sustainable development	5	5	0.814	0.662
X_9	Identify new sustainable development opportunities from emerging social expectations and environmental regulation	4	4	0.833	0.694
X_{10}	Provide adequate trainings to our employees regarding sustainable development	4	5	0.896	0.802
X_{11}	Experiment new clean technologies	4	4	0.925	0.856
X_{12}	Supporting employees to share good practices and new sustainable ideas	4	4	0.830	0.690
X_{13}	Cooperate with external partners in developing sustainable innovations	4	4	0.838	0.703
X_{14}	Acquire of machinery, facilities, and software to realize sustainable innovation projects	4	4	0.798	0.636

(*Continued*)

Table 3.2 (Continued)

Variable	*Description*	*Median*	*Mode*	*Std. Dev.*	*Variance*
X_{15}	Design strategic plans to systematically navigate the development of new sustainability initiative	4	4	0.794	0.631
X_{16}	Create dedicated teams to guide sustainability projects	4	4	1.018	1.036
Reconfiguring capabilities					
X_{17}	Evaluate the sustainable performance of our business operations	4	4	0.858	0.736
X_{18}	Improve our processes, products, and systems for sustainability	4	4	0.765	0.585
X_{19}	Balance our short-term economic benefits with long-term sustainable development goals	4	4	0.958	0.918
X_{20}	Managing internal factors that cause negative sustainable impacts	4	4	0.941	0.886
X_{21}	Perform auditing and risk analysis about the potential factors that cause environmental impacts	4	4	0.923	0.852
X_{22}	Increase our flexibility to increase the possibility of introducing new sustainability-oriented solutions	4	4	0.845	0.713

Note: Description of scale based on Karman and Savanevičienė (2021).

Project success (explained variables)

In the case of measuring the project's success, we decided to use a scale developed by Aga et al. (2016). It is based on a 14-statement describing various aspects of the project implementation success, that is, covering time, cost, performance, client use, satisfaction, and effectiveness ($P_1 - P_{14}$). The respondents assessed the items also on a Likert scale. The Cronbach's alpha was 0.812. The list of statements and descriptive statistics are presented in Table 3.4.

Method

We used the ordered logistic regression model to study the effect of the explanatory variables ($X_1 - X_{22}$) on the ordered explained variable ($Y_1 - Y_7$, $P_1 - P_{14}$). According to Winkelman and Boes, models for ordered dependent variables are usually motivated by an underlying continuous but latent process y_i^* given by:

Table 3.3 Environmental orientation – descriptive statistics

Variable	*Description*	*Median*	*Mode*	*Std. Dev.*	*Variance*
Internal environmental orientation					
Y_1	My company has a clear policy statement urging environmental awareness	4.0	5.0	0.965	0.931
Y_2	Environmental preservation is a high priority in my company	4.0	4.0	1.050	1.102
Y_3	Preserving the environment is a central value in my company	3.0	3.0	1.267	1.607
Y_4	My company promotes environmental preservation as a major company goal	3.0	3.0	1.272	1.617
External environmental orientation					
Y_5	My company has a responsibility to preserve the environment	4.0	5.0	1.146	1.312
Y_6	People expect my company to be environmentally conscious	4.0	4.0	0.994	0.989
Y_7	My company strives for an image of environmental responsibility	4.0	4.0	0.988	0.975

Note: Description of scale based on Gabler *et al.* (2015).

Table 3.4 Project success – descriptive statistics

Variable	*Description*	*Median*	*Mode*	*Std. Dev.*	*Variance*
P_1	The project was completed on time	5.0	5.0	0.687	0.472
P_2	The project was completed according to the budget allocated	4.0	4.0	0.798	0.637
P_3	The outcomes of the project are used by its intended end users	4.0	4.0	0.919	0.844
P_4	The outcomes of the project are likely to be sustained	4.0	4.0	1.010	1.021
P_5	The outcomes of the project have directly benefited the intended end users, either through increasing efficiency or effectiveness	4.0	4.0	0.825	0.680
P_6	Given the problem for which it was developed, the project seems to do the best job of solving that problem	4.0	5.0	0.854	0.729
P_7	I was satisfied with the process by which the project was implemented.	4.0	5.0	0.859	0.738

(*Continued*)

Table 3.4 (Continued)

Variable	*Description*	*Median*	*Mode*	*Std. Dev.*	*Variance*
P_8	Project team members were satisfied with the process by which the project was implemented	4.0	5.0	0.851	0.724
P_9	The project had no or minimal start-up problems because it was readily accepted by its end users.	4.0	4.0	1.016	1.031
P_{10}	The project has directly led to improved performance for the end users/target beneficiaries	4.0	4.0	0.711	0.506
P_{11}	The project has made a visible positive impact on the target beneficiaries	4.0	4.0	0.699	0.489
P_{12}	Project specifications were met by the time of handover to the target beneficiaries.	4.0	4.0	0.831	0.690
P_{13}	The target beneficiaries were satisfied with the outcomes of the project	4.0	5.0	0.779	0.607
P_{14}	Our principal donors were satisfied with the outcomes of the project implementation	4.0	5.0	0.805	0.648

Note: Description of scale based on Aga et al. (2016).

$$y_i^* = x_i^{'}\beta + u_i \quad i = 1,\dots,n \tag{3.1}$$

with the deterministic component $x_i'\beta$ (the linear index of regressors), and the random terms u_i, which are assumed to be independently and identically distributed with the distribution function $F(u)$ with a mean of zero and constant variance (Winkelmann and Boes, 2006).

For interpretation of the logit model estimation results, we used odds ratios (OR). If we mark the chance as:

$$\frac{p_i}{1-p_i} = \exp(x_i^{'}\beta) = exp(\beta_0 + \beta_1 X_{1i} + \beta_2 X_{2i} + \cdots + \beta_k X_{ki}) = \Omega(x_i), \tag{3.2}$$

is the variable X_{mi} increased by a unit and the odds without this increase equal:

$$\frac{\Omega(x_i^m, X_{mi}+1)}{\Omega(x_i^m, X_{mi})} = exp(\beta_m), \tag{3.3}$$

where x_i^m is the vector x_i without the variable X_{mi}. Formula (3.3) shows that an increase in the value of X_{mi} by one unit is related, *ceteris paribus*, with an $exp(\beta_m)$

-fold change in the OR. In the case of $exp(\beta_m) > 1$ we have an increase, and in the case of $exp(\beta_m) < 1$ we have a decrease in the OR.

We used the maximum likelihood estimation method and STATA.16.1 software to estimate all of the models.

Results

Firstly, we examined the possibility of a common method variance (CMV) bias. One-way Harman's test was verified by taking into account the explanatory and explained variables. The results showed that a single factor explains 26.8% of the variance in the case of SDA, 44.5% – of environmental orientation, and 29.8% – of project success. Consequently, according to Podsakoff et al. (2003), there is no CMV bias.

Next, we estimate the ordered logistic regression models and OR. The results in terms of the impact of SDA on environmental orientation are shown in Table 3.5, while in terms of the impact of SDA on the success of projects – in Table 3.6.

In terms of the impact of SDA on environmental orientation, the results (Table 3.5) indicate that all the estimated models ($Y_1 - Y_7$) are significant (*p*-value ≤ 0.0000). Therefore, the null hypothesis that the model is not significant was rejected in each case.

The results showed that in terms of SMEs' internal environmental orientation, only three variables related to the SDA are statistically significant factors affecting all its elements ($Y_1 - Y_4$). One of them belongs to scanning capabilities – X_6 – which uses the information about the emerging customer preference to guide the development of green market strategy; one to sensing capabilities – X_{11} – which experiments with new clean technologies; and one to reconfiguring capabilities – X_{21} – which performs auditing and risk analysis about the potential factors that cause environmental impacts. In turn, in the range of SMEs' external environmental orientation, none of the surveyed SDAs affected in a statistically significant way all the surveyed elements of external environmental orientation ($Y_5 - Y_7$).

The results presented in Table 3.6 indicate that not all of the estimated models were significant. In the case of the P_1 model, the null hypothesis that the model is not significant should be accepted (*p*-value ≤ 0.0496). In other cases, the estimated $P_2 - P_{14}$ models are statistically significant (*p*-value ≤ 0.0000). Therefore, the null hypothesis should be rejected.

Unfortunately, none of the analyzed SDAs were statistically significant for all the elements determining the project's success ($P_2 - P_{14}$). However, we believe this is due to many of its potential determinants (14-item scale).

Discussion of the findings

Answering the first research question – Do sustainable dynamic abilities positively influence the environmental orientation of SMEs? – it can be said that it is ambiguous. This is due to several reasons.

Table 3.5 Ordered logistic regression – sustainable dynamic capabilities and environmental orientation

Variables	*Internal environmental orientation*					
	Y_1		Y_2		Y_3	
	β	*OR*	β	*OR*	β	*OR*
X_1	−0.021	0.979	−0.304**	0.738**	−0.163	0.850
X_2	0.267**	1.306**	0.136	1.145	0.177	1.193
X_3	0.140	1.151	0.150	1.162	0.040	1.041
X_4	0.101	1.106	0.103	1.108	0.287***	1.332***
X_5	0.318***	1.374***	0.364***	1.439***	0.083	1.086
X_6	0.309***	1.362***	0.312***	1.366***	0.191**	1.210**
X_7	−0.279**	0.757**	−0.265**	0.767***	−0.207	0.813
X_8	0.240*	1.271*	0.174	1.190	−0.022	0.978
X_9	0.096	1.101	0.227*	1.255	−0.042	0.958
X_{10}	−0.142	0.868	−0.167	0.846	0.074	1.077
X_{11}	0.196**	1.217**	0.264***	1.303***	0.328***	1.388***
X_{12}	0.145	1.157	−0.163	0.850	0.044	1.045
X_{13}	−0.021	0.979	0.124	1.132	0.034	1.035
X_{14}	−0.022	0.978	−0.021	0.979	−0.257*	0.773*
X_{15}	0.055	1.057	0.130	1.139	0.156	1.169
X_{16}	−0.046	0.955	−0.125	0.882	0.116	1.123
X_{17}	0.108	1.114	0.047	1.049	0.013	1.013
X_{18}	−0.160	0.852	0.037	1.038	−0.127	0.881
X_{19}	0.182**	1.199**	0.079	1.082	0.085	1.089
X_{20}	−0.133	0.876	−0.024	0.976	−0.108	0.897
X_{21}	0.412***	1.509***	0.329***	1.390***	0.449***	1.566***
X_{22}	0.029	1.029	0.035	1.035	0.061	1.063
/cut1	2.529		1.698		2.573	
/cut2	4.077		3.408		3.909	
/cut3	5.894		4.680		5.277	
/cut4	7.739		6.578		6.620	
Log pseudolikelihood	−710.11		−757.08		−901.14	
Wald chi2(22)	133.79		136.35		138.32	
Prob > chi2	0.0000		0.0000		0.0000	
Pseudo R2	0.0936		0.0863		0.0716	

Note: *** *p*-value ≤0.01; ** *p*-value ≤ 0.05; * *p*-value ≤ 0.1.

Firstly, we used extended scales in our research. To measure the SDA, we applied the 22-statement DC scale developed by Karman and Savanevičienė (2021), in turn, to measure environmental orientation, the 7-statement scale developed by Banerjee (2001) was applied.

Secondly, as a result of separating environmental orientation into two types – internal and external, we were able to precisely determine the way in which SDA affects each of them. It turned out that a clearly positive impact can be observed only in the case of three types of SDA and internal environmental orientation.

External environmental orientation							
Y_4		Y_5		Y_6		Y_7	
β	*OR*	*β*	*OR*	*β*	*OR*	*β*	*OR*
−0.106	0.900	−0.020	0.981	−0.082	0.922	0.105	1.111
0.127	1.136	0.269**	1.308**	−0.059	0.942	−0.032	0.969
0.040	1.040	−0.039	0.962	−0.041	0.960	0.370***	1.448***
0.206**	1.228**	−0.040	0.960	−0.045	0.956	−0.084	0.919
0.128	1.136	0.194*	1.214*	0.241***	1.272***	0.164	1.178
0.162*	1.176*	0.212**	1.236**	0.087	1.091	0.312***	1.366***
−0.246**	0.782**	−0.222*	0.801*	−0.009	0.991	−0.224*	0.799*
−0.087	0.916	0.082	1.086	−0.067	0.935	0.053	1.055
−0.012	0.988	0.153	1.165	0.201*	1.223*	0.194*	1.214*
0.059	1.061	0.081	1.084	0.155	1.168	−0.052	0.949
0.161*	1.174*	0.126	1.134	−0.034	0.967	0.196**	1.216**
0.098	1.103	−0.010	0.990	0.016	1.016	−0.002	0.998
0.040	1.041	0.104	1.109	−0.026	0.975	0.148	1.160
−0.182	0.833	0.016	1.016	0.126	1.135	−0.056	0.945
0.161	1.175	0.019	1.019	−0.084	0.919	−0.165	0.848
0.142	1.152	−0.187*	0.829*	−0.188**	0.828**	−0.119	0.888
−0.027	0.974	0.049	1.050	0.150	1.162	0.039	1.040
−0.120	0.887	−0.064	0.938	−0.042	0.959	0.048	1.049
0.029	1.029	0.016	1.016	0.046	1.048	0.170*	1.185*
0.015	1.015	0.091	1.095	0.006	1.006	0.044	1.045
0.468***	1.598***	0.274**	1.315**	0.054	1.056	0.231**	1.260**
0.011	1.011	0.110	1.117	0.252**	1.286**	0.164	1.178
2.156		1.650		−0.906		2.135	
3.433		2.947		0.187		3.151	
4.835		4.161		1.673		4.699	
6.000		5.585		3.384		6.603	
−912.57		−825.71		−773.00		−726.93	
100.71		85.77		44.25		95.37	
0.0000		0.0000		0.0000		0.0000	
0.0577		0.0491		0.0264		0.0685	

One of them belongs to scanning capabilities – X_6 – which uses the information about the emerging customer preference to guide the development of green market strategy; one to sensing capabilities – X_{11} – which experiments with new clean technologies; and one to reconfiguring capabilities – X_{21} – which performs auditing and risk analysis about the potential factors that cause environmental impacts.

The results presented in Table 3.5 suggest that a higher assessment of the use of information about the emerging customer preference to guide the development of a green market strategy (X_6) increases the chance that the company has a clear

Table 3.6 Ordered logistic regression – sustainable dynamic capabilities and project success

Variables	P_1		P_2		P_3	
	β	*OR*	β	*OR*	β	*OR*
X_1	0.062	1.064	0.145	1.156	0.044	1.045
X_2	0.174	1.191	−0.022	0.978	0.276**	1.317**
X_3	−0.097	0.907	0.038	1.039	−0.209*	0.812*
X_4	0.063	1.065	0.186**	1.204**	−0.005	0.995
X_5	−0.048	0.953	−0.043	0.958	0.076	1.079
X_6	0.064	1.066	0.083	1.086	0.045	1.046
X_7	−0.087	0.917	0.020	1.020	0.095	1.100
X_8	−0.108	0.897	0.046	1.047	−0.201	0.818
X_9	0.124	1.132	−0.045	0.956	−0.038	0.962
X_{10}	−0.200*	0.819*	−0.138	0.871	−0.047	0.954
X_{11}	0.180	1.197	−0.094	0.910	0.044	1.045
X_{12}	0.014	1.014	−0.064	0.938	0.031	1.031
X_{13}	0.342***	1.407***	0.023	1.023	0.015	1.015
X_{14}	−0.008	0.992	0.312**	1.366**	0.456***	1.578***
X_{15}	0.102	1.107	−0.049	0.953	−0.029	0.972
X_{16}	0.141	1.151	0.019	1.019	0.222**	1.248**
X_{17}	0.160	1.173	0.311***	1.364***	0.092	1.097
X_{18}	−0.008	0.992	−0.014	0.986	0.195	1.215
X_{19}	−0.091	0.913	0.256***	1.292***	0.015	1.015
X_{20}	−0.152	0.859	−0.105	0.901	0.004	1.004
X_{21}	0.154	1.166	0.219**	1.245**	0.115	1.122
X_{22}	−1.338	1.064	0.070	1.073	0.237**	1.267**
/cut1	0.122		−0.671		0.614	
/cut2	1.315		1.063		3.148	
/cut3	3.638		2.999		4.568	
/cut4	0.062		5.389		6.730	
Log pseudolikelihood	−506.25		−664.85		−727.11	
Wald chi2(22)	33.95		61.91		76.90	
Prob > chi2	0.0496		0.0000		0.0000	
Pseudo R2	0.0466		0.0465		0.0597	

Note: *** *p*-value ≤ 0.01; ** *p*-value ≤ 0.05; * *p*-value ≤ 0.1.

policy statement urging environmental awareness (Y_1) by 36.2%, that environmental preservation is a high priority in the company (Y_2) by 36.6%, that preserving the environment is a central value in the company (Y_3) by 21%, and that the company promotes environmental preservation as a major company goal (Y_4) by 17.6%. A higher assessment of the experiments with new clean technologies (X_{11}) increases the chance that the company has a clear policy statement urging environmental awareness (Y_1) by 21.7%, that environmental preservation is a high priority in the company (Y_2) by 30.3%, that preserving the environment is a central value in the company (Y_3) by 38.8%, and that the company promotes environmental preservation

P_4		P_5		P_6		P_7	
β	*OR*	β	*OR*	β	*OR*	β	*OR*
0.077	1.080	0.235*	1.264*	0.154	1.166	0.024	1.025
0.069	1.071	0.058	1.060	0.145	1.156	0.340**	1.405**
0.058	1.060	0.110	1.116	0.229*	1.257*	0.049	1.050
0.121	1.129	0.065	1.067	0.074	1.077	0.061	1.063
−0.157*	0.855*	0.069	1.071	0.108	1.114	0.134	1.144
0.008	1.008	−0.037	0.964	−0.133	0.876	0.075	1.078
0.043	1.044	−0.050	0.951	0.048	1.049	−0.018	0.982
−0.122	0.885	−0.194	0.824	−0.004	0.996	0.031	1.031
−0.241**	0.786**	0.226*	1.254*	0.124	1.132	0.131	1.139
0.045	1.046	0.002	1.002	−0.006	0.994	−0.072	0.930
0.118	1.125	0.038	1.038	−0.018	0.982	0.071	1.074
0.061	1.063	−0.167	0.846	−0.054	0.947	0.337***	1.401***
0.060	1.062	0.205*	1.228*	0.057	1.059	0.062	1.063
0.195	1.215	0.299**	1.348**	0.281**	1.325**	0.179	1.196
−0.074	0.928	0.169	1.184	0.061	1.063	−0.039	0.962
0.175*	1.191*	−0.014	0.986	−0.040	0.961	0.124	1.132
0.056	1.058	0.129	1.138	0.094	1.099	0.180*	1.197*
0.001	1.001	0.211	1.235	0.152	1.164	0.066	1.069
0.268***	1.308***	0.228**	1.256**	0.195**	1.216**	−0.078	0.925
−0.014	0.986	−0.075	0.927	0.100	1.105	0.178*	1.195*
0.115	1.122	0.013	1.013	0.032	1.033	−0.230**	0.794**
0.206**	1.228**	0.268**	1.307**	0.020	1.020	0.138	1.148
−0.188		2.307		0.957		2.482	
2.041		3.723		3.382		3.687	
3.783		5.358		5.021		5.186	
5.348		7.872		7.019		7.383	
−813.52		−643.25		−675.36		−642.94	
64.68		87.45		63.37		78.93	
0.0000		0.0000		0.0000		0.0000	
0.0409		0.0742		0.0542		0.0703	

as a major company goal (Y_4) by 17.4%. Finally in the case of a higher assessment of performing audit and risk analysis about the potential factors that cause environmental impacts (X_{21}) increases the chance that the company has a clear policy statement urging environmental awareness (Y_1) by 50.9%, that environmental preservation is a high priority in the company (Y_2) by 39%, that preserving the environment is a central value in the company (Y_3) by 56.6%, and that the company promotes environmental preservation as a major company goal (Y_4) by 59.8%. Looking from this perspective, the internal environmental orientation of the company is most positively influenced by the SDA belonging to the ability to reconfigure resources (X_{21}).

Table 3.6 (Continued)

Variables	P_8		P_9		P_{10}	
	β	*OR*	β	*OR*	β	*OR*
X_1	0.271**	1.311**	−0.006	0.994	0.046	1.047
X_2	0.098	1.102	0.133	1.142	−0.014	0.986
X_3	−0.052	0.950	0.039	1.040	0.058	1.059
X_4	0.133	1.143	0.161*	1.175*	−0.034	0.966
X_5	0.080	1.083	−0.195**	0.823**	0.103	1.109
X_6	0.118	1.125	−0.025	0.975	−0.036	0.965
X_7	−0.045	0.956	0.064	1.067	0.254*	1.289*
X_8	−0.020	0.980	−0.223**	0.800**	−0.291*	0.743*
X_9	−0.079	0.924	−0.079	0.924	0.106	1.111
X_{10}	0.056	1.058	−0.108	0.898	0.130	1.139
X_{11}	−0.002	0.998	0.120	1.128	0.117	1.124
X_{12}	0.375***	1.455***	−0.006	0.994	−0.049	0.952
X_{13}	−0.002	0.998	0.085	1.089	0.242**	1.274**
X_{14}	0.154	1.167	0.138	1.148	0.226*	1.253*
X_{15}	0.103	1.109	0.347***	1.415***	−0.096	0.908
X_{16}	0.045	1.046	0.087	1.090	0.138	1.148
X_{17}	0.226*	1.253*	0.223**	1.250**	−0.015	0.985
X_{18}	0,117	1,125	0,227**	1,255**	0,347**	1,415**
X_{19}	−0,066	0,936	0,041	1,042	0,126	1,134
X_{20}	0,099	1,104	0,112	1,119	0,057	1,059
X_{21}	−0,047	0,95a4	0,135	1,144	0,111	1,118
X_{22}	0,133	1,142	−0,012	0,988	0,168	1,183
/cut1	2,358		1,122		0,584	
/cut2	3,501		3,084		2,543	
/cut3	4,951		4,823		4,621	
/cut4	7,172		6,596		7,513	
Log pseudolikelihood	−638.84		−820.43		−583.62	
Wald chi2(22)	67.62		78.93		71.64	
Prob > chi2	0.0000		0.0000		0.0000	
Pseudo R2	0.0667		0.0482		0.0734	

Note: *** *p*-value ≤0.01; ** *p*-value ≤ 0.05; * *p*-value ≤ 0.1.

In the case of the SDA's impact on the company's external environmental orientation, the results presented in Table 3.5 indicate an ambiguous trend. Firstly, none of the surveyed SDAs influenced all external manifestations of the company's environmental orientation ($Y_5 – Y_7$). Only six SDAs (X_5, X_6, X_7, X_9, X_{16}, and X_{21}) affected two simultaneously. Among them, the strongest was observed in the case of X_6 – its higher score will increase the chances that the company strives for an image of environmental responsibility (Y_7) by 36.6% and X_{21} – its higher score will increase the chances that the company has a responsibility to preserve the environment (Y_5) by 31.5%. Secondly, this impact was negative in the case of X_7 and X_{16}. So, a higher assessment of the environment for the development of

P_{11}		P_{12}		P_{13}		P_{14}	
β	*OR*	β	*OR*	β	*OR*	β	*OR*
0.080	1.083	−0.004	0.996	0.057	1.058	0.163	1.177
−0.008	0.992	−0.084	0.919	0.186	1.204	−0.117	0.890
0.035	1.036	0.402***	1.495***	0.118	1.125	0.131	1.139
0.052	1.053	0.117	1.124	−0.002	0.998	0.203**	1.225**
0.206**	1.229**	−0.045	0.956	0.011	1.011	−0.084	0.919
0.070	1.072	0.116	1.123	0.098	1.103	0.243**	1.275**
0.084	1.088	−0.051	0.950	0.141	1.151	0.052	1.054
0.049	1.050	−0.042	0.959	−0.035	0.965	0.064	1.066
0.137	1.147	0.050	1.052	0.189	1.208	−0.044	0.957
−0.033	0.967	0.156	1.169	0.114	1.120	0.139	1.149
0.024	1.024	0.092	1.097	0.001	1.001	−0.198**	0.820**
−0.009	0.991	−0.071	0.932	0.003	1.003	0.173	1.189
0.274**	1.315**	0.213*	1.237*	0.167	1.182	−0.015	0.985
0.373***	1.452***	0.246*	1.279*	0.236**	1.266**	0.051	1.052
−0.182	0.833	−0.060	0.942	−0.092	0.912	−0.037	0.964
0.045	1.046	0.098	1.103	−0.031	0.970	0.194**	1.214**
0.106	1.111	0.052	1.054	0.363***	1.438***	0.181*	1.198*
0,027	1,028	−0,027	0,974	0,074	1,077	−0,122	0,885
0,139	1,149	0,166	1,181	−0,035	0,965	0,066	1,068
0,140	1,150	0,123	1,131	0,119	1,126	0,041	1,042
−0,173	0,841	−0,025	0,975	−0,188*	0,829*	0,017	1,017
0,323***	1,382***	0,093	1,098	0,162	1,176	0,187*	1,205*
1,324		1,087		1,338		−0,511	
2,111		2,547		3,011		1,592	
4,703		4,677		4,606		3,120	
7,424		6,957		6,980		5,317	
−557.51		−681.26		−607.29		−628.32	
71.77		62.98		61.38		68.98	
0.0000		0.0000		0.0000		0.0000	
0.0809		0.0585		0.0649		0.0587	

sustainable innovations (X_7) decreases the chance that the company has a responsibility to preserve the environment (Y_5) by 19.9% and that the company strives for an image of environment responsibility (Y_7) by 20.1%. In turn, a higher assessment of the creation of dedicated teams to guide sustainability projects (X_{16}) decreases the chance that the company has a responsibility to preserve the environment (Y_5) by 17.1% and that the people expect the company to be environmentally conscious (Y_6) by 17.2%.

For the second research question, whether sustainable DC positively influence the success of SME projects, the answer is more straightforward. None of the surveyed SDAs affected all aspects of project success at the same time ($P_1 - P_{14}$).

However, it is worth emphasizing that in the case of one SDA, namely the purchase of machinery, equipment, and software for the purpose of implementing sustainable innovative projects (sensing capability [X_{14}] a statistical significance was observed in the case of eight manifestations of project success. As a consequence, it can be stated that a higher assessment of this ability increases the chances that:

- the project was completed according to the budget allocated (P_2) by 36.6%,
- the outcomes of the project are used by its intended end users (P_3) by 57.8%,
- the outcomes of the project have directly benefited the intended end users, either through increased efficiency or effectiveness (P_5) by 34.8%,
- given the problem for which it was developed, the project seems to do the best job of solving that problem (P_6) by 32.5%,
- the project has directly led to improved performance for the end users/target beneficiaries (P_{10}) by 25.3%,
- the project has made a visible positive impact on the target beneficiaries (P_{11}) by 45.2%
- project specifications were met by the time of handover to the target beneficiaries (P_{12}) by 27.9%.
- the target beneficiaries were satisfied with the outcomes of the project (P_{13}) by 26.6%.

Other SDAs that turned out to be statistically significant in more manifestations of project success are two reconfigurable capabilities, i.e., X_{17} – evaluate the sustainable performance of our business operations (P_2, P_7, P_8, P_9, P_{13}, P_{14}) and X_{22} – increase our flexibility to increase the possibility of introducing new sustainability-oriented solutions (P_3, P_4, P_5, P_{11}, P_{14}).

In conclusion, three issues are worth noting. Firstly, SDAs have a positive impact on the internal environmental orientation of the surveyed SMEs. Secondly, the impact of the SDA on the external environmental orientation of the surveyed SMEs turned out to be ambiguous. Thirdly, SDAs do not affect all aspects of project success. The above leads to suggesting further research in these areas, both in large enterprises and from the international perspective.

References

Aboelmaged, M. (2018), "Direct and indirect effects of eco-innovation, environmental orientation and supplier collaboration on hotel performance: An empirical study", *Journal of Cleaner Production*, Vol. 184, pp. 537–549.

Aga, D.A., Noorderhaven, N. and Vallejo, B. (2016), "Transformational leadership and project success: The mediating role of team-building", *International Journal of Project Management*, Vol. 34 No. 5, pp. 806–818.

Agyabeng-Mensah, Y., Baah, C., Afum, E. and Kumi, C.A. (2023), "Circular supply chain practices and corporate sustainability performance: do ethical supply chain leadership and environmental orientation make a difference?", *Journal of Manufacturing Technology Management*, available at: https://doi.org/10.1108/JMTM-08-2022-0296.

Albert, M., Balve, P. and Spang, K. (2017), "Evaluation of project success: a structured literature review", *International Journal of Managing Projects in Business*, Vol. 10 No. 4, pp. 796–821.

Alvarenga, J.C., Branco, R.R., Guedes, A.L.A., Soares, C.A.P. and Silva, W. da S. e. (2019), "The project manager core competencies to project success", *International Journal of Managing Projects in Business*, Vol. 13 No. 2, pp. 277–292.

Amui, L.B.L., Jabbour, C.J.C., de Sousa Jabbour, A.B.L. and Kannan, D. (2017), "Sustainability as a dynamic organizational capability: A systematic review and a future agenda toward a sustainable transition", *Journal of Cleaner Production*, Vol. 142, pp. 308–322.

Badrinarayanan, V., Ramachandran, I. and Madhavaram, S. (2019), "Resource orchestration and dynamic managerial capabilities: Focusing on sales managers as effective resource orchestrators", *Journal of Personal Selling and Sales Management, Routledge*, Vol. 39 No. 1, pp. 23–41.

Banerjee, S.B. (2001), "Managerial perceptions of corporate environmentalism: Interpretations from industry and strategic implications for organizations", *Journal of Management Studies*, Vol. 38 No. 4, pp. 489–513.

Banerjee, S.B. (2002), "Corporate environmentalism: The construct and its measurement", *Journal of Business Research*, Vol. 55 No. 3, pp. 177–191.

Bergmann, T. and Karwowski, W. (2019), "Agile project management and project success: A literature review", *Advances in Intelligent Systems and Computing*, Vol. 783, pp. 405–414.

Beske, P. (2012), "Dynamic capabilities and sustainable supply chain management", *International Journal of Physical Distribution and Logistics Management*, Vol. 42 No. 4, pp. 372–387.

Beske, P., Land, A. and Seuring, S. (2014), "Sustainable supply chain management practices and dynamic capabilities in the food industry: A critical analysis of the literature", *International Journal of Production Economics, Elsevier*, Vol. 152, pp. 131–143.

Borland, H., Ambrosini, V., Lindgreen, A. and Vanhamme, J. (2016), "Building theory at the intersection of ecological sustainability and strategic management", *Journal of Business Ethics*, Vol. 135 No. 2, pp. 293–307.

Chan, R.Y.K., He, H., Chan, H.K. and Wang, W.Y.C. (2012), "Environmental orientation and corporate performance: The mediation mechanism of green supply chain management and moderating effect of competitive intensity", *Industrial Marketing Management*, Vol. 41 No. 4, pp. 621–630.

Chan, R.Y.K. and Ma, K.H.Y. (2016), "Environmental orientation of exporting SMEs from an emerging economy: Its antecedents and consequences", *Management International Review*, Vol. 56 No. 5, pp. 597–632.

Chavez, R., Malik, M., Ghaderi, H. and Yu, W. (2021), "Environmental orientation, external environmental information exchange and environmental performance: Examining mediation and moderation effects", *International Journal of Production Economics*, Vol. 240, available at: https://doi.org/10.1016/j.ijpe.2021.108222.

Chen, Y.-S. and Chang, C.-H. (2013), "The determinants of green product development performance: Green dynamic capabilities, green transformational leadership, and green creativity", *Journal of Business Ethics*, Vol. 116 No. 1, pp. 107–119.

Dangelico, R.M., Pujari, D. and Pontrandolfo, P. (2017), "Green product innovation in manufacturing firms: A sustainability-oriented dynamic capability perspective", *Business Strategy and the Environment*, Vol. 26 No. 4, pp. 490–506.

Dentoni, D., Bitzer, V. and Pascucci, S. (2016), "Cross-Sector partnerships and the co-creation of dynamic capabilities for stakeholder orientation", *Journal of Business Ethics*, Vol. 135 No. 1, pp. 35–53.

Eisenhardt, K.M. and Martin, J.A. (2000), "Dynamic capabilities: What are they?", *Strategic Management Journal*, Vol. 21 No. 10–11, pp. 1105–1121.

Emiliano de Souza, D., Favoretto, C. and Carvalho, M.M. (2022), "Knowledge management, absorptive and dynamic capacities and project success: A review and framework", *EMJ – Engineering Management Journal*, Vol. 34 No. 1, pp. 50–69.

Ettlie et al. (2023). https://doi.org/10.1109/TEM.2020.3045650

Fabrizio, C.M., Kaczam, F., de Moura, G.L., da Silva, L.S.C.V., da Silva, W.V. and da Veiga, C.P. (2022), "Competitive advantage and dynamic capability in small and medium-sized enterprises: A systematic literature review and future research directions", *Review of Managerial Science*, Vol. 16 No. 3, pp. 617–648.

Ferreira, J., Cardim, S. and Coelho, A. (2021), "Dynamic capabilities and mediating effects of innovation on the competitive advantage and firm's performance: The moderating role of organizational learning capability", *Journal of the Knowledge Economy*, Vol. 12 No. 2, pp. 620–644.

Ferreira, J. and Coelho, A. (2020), "Dynamic capabilities, innovation and branding capabilities and their impact on competitive advantage and SME's performance in Portugal: The moderating effects of entrepreneurial orientation", *International Journal of Innovation Science*, Vol. 12 No. 3, pp. 255–286.

Fraj-Andrés, E., Martinez-Salinas, E. and Matute-Vallejo, J. (2009), "A multidimensional approach to the influence of environmental marketing and orientation on the firm's organizational performance", *Journal of Business Ethics*, Vol. 88 No. 2, pp. 263–286.

Gabler, C.B., Richey, R.G. and Rapp, A. (2015), "Developing an eco-capability through environmental orientation and organizational innovativeness", *Industrial Marketing Management*, Vol. 45 No. 1, pp. 151–161.

GUS. (2023), "Local Data Bank of GUS". https://bdl.stat.gov.pl/bdl/start

Helfat, C.E., Finkelstein, S., Mitchell, W., Peteraf, M., Singh, H., Teece, D.J. and Winter, S.G. (2007), *Dynamic Capabilities: Understanding Strategic Change in Organizations*, 1 edition, Wiley-Blackwell.

Hermano, V. and Martín-Cruz, N. (2016), "The role of top management involvement in firms performing projects: A dynamic capabilities approach", *Journal of Business Research*, Vol. 69 No. 9, pp. 3447–3458.

Hermano, V., Martin-Cruz, N. and Pajares, J. (2022), "The effect of project management dynamic capabilities on firm performance", *Baltic Journal of Management*, Vol. 17 No. 2, pp. 266–284.

Karman, A. and Savanevičienė, A. (2021), "Enhancing dynamic capabilities to improve sustainable competitiveness: Insights from research on organisations of the Baltic region", *Baltic Journal of Management, Emerald Group Holdings Ltd.*, Vol. 16 No. 2, pp. 318–341.

Khan, K.A., Turner, J.R. and Maqsood, T. (2013), "*Factors that influence the success of public sector projects in Pakistan*", Proceedings of IRNOP 2013 Conference, June 17–19, 2013, No. JUNE, pp. 1–25.

Lee, S.Y.D., Weiner, B.J., Harrison, M.I. and Belden, C.M. (2013), "Organizational transformation: A systematic review of empirical research in health care and other industries", *Medical Care Research and Review*, Vol. 70 No. 2, pp. 115–142.

Leifer, R. (1989), "Understanding organizational transformation using a dissipative structure model", *Human Relations*, Vol. 42 No. 10, pp. 899–916.

McNulty, T. and Ferlie, E. (2011), "Reengineering Health Care: The Complexities of Organizational Transformation", in McNulty, T. and Ferlie, E. (Eds.), *Reengineering Health Care: The Complexities of Organizational Transformation*, Oxford University Press, London, pp. 1–404.

Mohd Naim Yassien, E. and Jumaa Alnajjar, F. (2020), "The impact of organization's dynamic capabilities on information systems project's success in the Jordanian telecommunication sector", *International Journal of Business and Management*, Vol. 15 No. 4, p. 138.

Müller, R. (2019), "The relationship between project governance and project success", in Joslin, R. (Ed.), *Project Management Methodologies, Governance and Success*, CRC Press Taylor & Francis Group, New York, pp. 141–170.

Niemi, E. and Pekkola, S. (2020), "The benefits of enterprise architecture in organizational transformation", *Business and Information Systems Engineering*, Vol. 62 No. 6, pp. 585–597.

Oliveira-Dias, D., Kneipp, J.M., Bichueti, R.S. and Gomes, C.M. (2022), "Fostering business model innovation for sustainability: A dynamic capabilities perspective", *Management Decision*, Vol. 60 No. 13, pp. 105–129.

Ozgul, B. (2022), "Does green transformational leadership develop green absorptive capacity? The role of internal and environmental orientation", *Systems*, Vol. 10 No. 6, available at: https://doi.org/10.3390/systems10060224

Pérez Rave, J.I., Guerrero, R.F., Vallina, A.S. and Echavarría, F.G. (2022), "Critical thinking, dynamic capabilities, and project performance: Empirical evidence in the continuous improvement project domain", *Total Quality Management and Business Excellence*, available at: https://doi.org/10.1080/14783363.2022.2111994

Podsakoff, P.M., MacKenzie, S.B., Lee, J.Y. and Podsakoff, N.P. (2003), "Common method biases in behavioral research: A critical review of the literature and recommended remedies", *Journal of Applied Psychology*, Vol. 88 No. 5, pp. 879–903.

Qiu, L., Jie, X., Wang, Y. and Zhao, M. (2020), "Green product innovation, green dynamic capability, and competitive advantage: Evidence from Chinese manufacturing enterprises", *Corporate Social Responsibility and Environmental Management*, Vol. 27 No. 1, pp. 146–165.

Saleem, F., Qureshi, S.S. and Malik, M.I. (2021), "Impact of environmental orientation on proactive and reactive environmental strategies: Mediating role of business environmental commitment", *Sustainability (Switzerland)*, Vol. 13 No. 15, available at: https://doi.org/10.3390/su13158361

Salvador, R.O. and Burciaga, A. (2020), "Organizational environmental orientation and employee environmental in-role behaviors: A cross-level study", *Business Ethics*, Vol. 29 No. 1, pp. 98–113.

Schilke, O., Hu, S. and Helfat, C.E. (2018), "Quo vadis, dynamic capabilities? A content-analytic review of the current state of knowledge and recommendations for future research", *Academy of Management Annals, Routledge*, Vol. 12 No. 1, pp. 390–439.

Scott-Young, C. and Samson, D. (2008), "Project success and project team management: Evidence from capital projects in the process industries", *Journal of Operations Management*, Vol. 26 No. 6, pp. 749–766.

Statistics Poland. (2023), "*REGON*", Bulletin of Public Information.

Teece, D.J., Pisano, G. and Shuen, A. (1997), "Dynamic capabilities and strategic management", *Strategic Management Journal*, Vol. 18 No. 7, pp. 509–533.

Winkelmann, R. and Boes, S. (2006), *Analysis of Microdata*, Springer, Berlin.

Wu, Q., He, Q. and Duan, Y. (2014), "Dynamic capabilities for CSR management: towards identifying common processes", *Society and Business Review, Emerald*, Vol. 9 No. 3, pp. 276–297.

Zameer, H., Wang, Y., Yasmeen, H. and Mubarak, S. (2022), "Green innovation as a mediator in the impact of business analytics and environmental orientation on green competitive advantage", *Management Decision*, Vol. 60 No. 2, pp. 488–507.

Zhou, C., Xia, W., Feng, T., Jiang, J. and He, Q. (2020), "How environmental orientation influences firm performance: The missing link of green supply chain integration", *Sustainable Development*, Vol. 28 No. 4, pp. 685–696.

4 Sustainable project management by considering the impact of modern technologies on stakeholder management

Seweryn Spałek

Industry 4.0 and project management—from the theoretical perspective

Project management these days is inextricably linked to an agile and a sustainable approach to running projects. It should be emphasized that stakeholders play a key role in both concepts. In addition, regardless of the industry, projects today or in the near future are closely linked to the application of modern technologies in enterprises, which is becoming synonymous with the fourth industrial revolution also referred to as Industry 4.0. Hence, this article will discuss the impact of Industry 4.0 on stakeholder management in projects.

The fourth industrial revolution derives from the term "Industry 4.0" and is conceptually related to it. The term was first used in early 2011 at the Hanover Science and Technology Fair. At that time, the government of the Federal Republic of Germany launched a strategic initiative that was referred to as "Industrie 4.0" (Industry 4.0) (Kagermann, Lukas, and Wahlster 2011). In its initial conception, this decision was intended to strengthen the competitiveness of the German manufacturing sector with a special focus on the machinery industry in the world. It should be mentioned that the machinery industry has been the backbone of the German economy for many years. It is estimated that its share in gross domestic product fluctuates around 25% and generates (directly and indirectly) half of the jobs in Germany (Federal Statistical Office 2020). To maintain and ultimately strengthen the existing competitive advantage of the German economy in the era of digital business transformation, a new global strategy was needed. Thus, in 2014, Industry 4.0 was integrated into a broader project called "High-Tech Strategies 2020" aimed at defining technical, economic, and sociopolitical assumptions for implementing industrial change that should result in economy's growing importance in global markets. As the assumptions of the "Industrie 4.0" concept are universal in nature (Faul, Jazdi, and Weyrich 2016), over time this has spread initially in Europe and then to the rest of the globe as the English-language "Industry 4.0" (Ganzarain and Errasti 2016; Qin, Liu, and Grosvenor 2016; Sanders, Elangeswaran, and Wulfsberg 2016).

Conducted literature study shows that the number of published articles from 2014 to 2022 indexed in the Web of Science Core Collection database, on Industry 4.0 topic has increased significantly. It should be noted that during 2014–2022

DOI: 10.4324/9781003356059-5

the share of publications from the area of management in the total number of publications on Industry 4.0 steadily increased. In the analyzed period their percentage share increased more than fivefold, which, considering the general upward trend of all publications on Industry 4.0, testifies to a definite strengthening of this issue in the research area of management sciences. It also shows that we are dealing with an increase in awareness of the impact of technologies underlying Industry 4.0 on managerial aspects of company operations, which translates into increasing research activity of people dealing with management issues in scientific centers from all over the world. The studied articles showed the increase in publications in 2014–2022 referring to Industry 4.0 clearly prove that this topic is important and topical and is significantly gaining in popularity from year to year among researchers publishing in internationally recognized journals. This observation also applies to issues narrowed down to the area of management, with particular emphasis on project management in Industry 4.0.

Identifying enablers of the fourth industrial revolution

Despite the passage of time, successive authors have stressed and emphasized that Industry 4.0 is still a matter of the future (Wang & Shang 2023), which, however, will undoubtedly happen sooner or later. This causes this concept to remain largely undefined. Although, as it has been already emphasized, with the lack of consensus among authors of publications as to the commonly accepted definition of the fourth industrial revolution in recent years, researchers have unanimously noted that enablers (of a technological nature) of the fourth industrial revolution are inevitably associated with Industry 4.0. This theme should be considered relevant to the subject matter undertaken in the monograph, as the following research question could have been formulated based thereon: What is the impact of Industry 4.0 enablers on project management with a special focus on stakeholders? It is important to emphasize that these enablers are already starting to occur in business practice and can therefore be used in empirical research in companies. Therefore, further consideration has been directed toward identifying the enablers of the fourth industrial revolution.

Jean-Charles André (2019), in a wide-ranging study on Industry 4.0, states that the world is undergoing continuous digitization with its accompanying global networks. However, these changes are taking place in a non-linear manner and, as a result, their consequences in a broader (not only technological) sense are difficult to determine. Industry 4.0 fits into this logic, as the possible effects of rapid technological development are multi-threaded and change over time. At the same time, in line with the prediction trend of the fourth industrial revolution, it presents a number of technological trends that are the basis for the existence of Industry 4.0. The first of these is *artificial intelligence* (AI) and machine learning, which are increasingly entering the present reality, and in some areas are omnipresent in financial analysis and approval of credit applications in banks, or virtual personal assistants in smartphones. The following are components of AI: collection and processing of *big data*, *Internet of Things* (IoT), *cloud computing*, neural networks, and processes in which artificial intelligence learns to perform tasks that are natural to the human brain (*deep learning*). The next technological trend is *scalability*, i.e., the ability to instantly resize a product or system according to current demand while maintaining functionality and quality, even in case of high-demand market. Furthermore, there will be *complexity*, associated with increasing levels of automation in manufacturing systems. The *digitization of production* will increase through the introduction of information systems for production planning and management. Other technological trends include the *automation* of data, production line and machinery management systems, and *automated data exchange* enabled by linking manufacturing sites in a global supply chain network.

A similar set of Industry 4.0 enablers is identified by Alexadre Moeuf with co-authors (2019), emphasizing: *Big data* and analytics; simulations; autonomous robots; IoT; cyber-physical systems; virtual reality; machine-to-machine communication; cyber security.

Athos Pacchini with co-authors (2019) reviewed the literature, in which he identified eight enablers of Industry 4.0, namely: IoT; big data; cloud computing; cyber-physical system (CPS); additive manufacturing; autonomous robots; augmented reality; artificial intelligence.

The different nature of technological factors and the need to group them is pointed out by Yubao Chen (2017). He distinguishes ten main technologies, which he identifies as key elements of Industry 4.0 and divides them into *integrated* and *intelligent*. In the first group he includes: *big data*, cloud computing, incremental manufacturing, automated robotics and IoT. In the second: the use of information systems, mobile devices, virtual reality, the industrial Internet, and cyber physical systems. He also makes the important observation that as a result of the implementation of the Industry 4.0 concept, we are facing a new trend of a shift from an information focus to a knowledge-based paradigm in which big data analytics and knowledge bases play a significant role.

It should be noted that cyber physical systems and IoT are mentioned as the most important technological factors by authors of also more recent studies (Liao et al., 2017; Rüßmann et al., 2015). Such an approach, while understandable from the point of view of technical sciences, cannot be accepted in the broader understanding of Industry 4.0. This is due to the fact that also other technological factors can have a significant impact on other than technical spheres of a company's activity. Thus, in order to capture as fully as possible the implications of the fourth industrial revolution in the area of management, it was decided not to focus exclusively on cyber physical systems and IoT. Therefore, an attempt was made to identify the enablers of the fourth industrial revolution on the basis of an analysis on articles and peer-reviewed conference materials indexed in the Web of Science database. The objective of this quantitative study was to verify and, if necessary, complement previous considerations based on a qualitative analysis of the text of selected articles dealing with the topic of these factors. In the first step, all possible keywords assigned to the analyzed publications from the field of Industry 4.0 were noted. As a result, a list of keywords was obtained. They were subsequently ranked in terms of frequency of occurrence in all publications. In the next step, an

Table 4.1 List of pre-selected enablers of the fourth industrial revolution, in alphabetical order

No.	*Enabler of the fourth industrial revolution*
1.	Additive manufacturing
2.	Artificial intelligence
3.	Augmented reality
4.	Automated data exchange
5.	Automation
6.	Autonomous robots
7.	Big data
8.	Cloud computing
9.	Cyber physical systems (CPS)
10.	Cyber security
11.	Data analytics
12.	Deep learning
13.	Digital twins
14.	Internet of Things (IoT)
15.	Simulation
16.	Virtual reality (VR)

attempt was made to identify these keywords that can be aggregated and assigned to a single term. For example: "Cyber physical systems" were written in keywords as "cyber physical systems", "cyber-physical production systems", "cyber physical system", "cyber-physical production systems (CPPS)", "cyber-physical systems (CPS)", "cyber-physical system (CPS)", "CPS", "cyberphysical systems", and "cyber-physical production system". As a result of the steps taken, they have been aggregated into a single term, namely "cyber physical systems". A similar method was adopted for the remaining keywords. Keywords that did not relate to technological factors were also eliminated, e.g., *consumer, marketing, model checking, survey, x-ray, x generation, xml, y generation, zero-energy standby, zlin region.*

As a result of the actions taken based on quantitative and qualitative research, a preliminary list of 16 enablers of the fourth industrial revolution was obtained (Table 4.1).

Analyzing the dependency network of the enablers of the fourth industrial revolution, it was observed that the automated data exchange factor does not occur jointly with any other factor in the analyzed publications. Therefore, it was excluded from further consideration. Thus, the enablers of the fourth industrial revolution finally closed in the number of 15 (Table 4.2).

Research method

Empirical research was carried out using a questionnaire survey. The research sample consisted of enterprises where New Product Development (NPD) projects are executed. To reach such a target group of respondents, a database of enterprises obtained in the previously conducted research funded by the National Science

Table 4.2 List of final selected enablers of the fourth industrial revolution, in alphabetical order

No.	*Enabler of the fourth industrial revolution*
1.	Additive manufacturing
2.	Artificial intelligence
3.	Augmented reality
4.	Automation
5.	Autonomous robots
6.	Big data
7.	Cloud computing
8.	Cyber physical systems
9.	Cyber security
10.	Data analytics
11.	Deep learning
12.	Digital twins
13.	Internet of Things (IoT)
14.	Simulation
15.	Virtual reality

Center was used (international research was conducted by the author under NCN grant N504 678740). Moreover, the invitation to participate in the research was disseminated using electronic communication channels in cooperation with the Project Management Institute and the International Project Management Association. Due to the assumed international nature, the research was conducted exclusively in English.

The adopted research model (Figure 4.1) assumed a stage of preliminary research in order to reach the target group of enterprises implementing NPD projects and to obtain information from them regarding the occurrence of enablers of the fourth industrial revolution. The questionnaire as a whole was accompanied by a metric indicating the type of projects implemented in the enterprise and the sector of activity, the size of employment, turnover, and the country (headquarters of the company). The goal of the preliminary research was to identify those enterprises in which all of the 15 previously identified enablers of Industry 4.0 were present and which are conducting NPD projects. To them was addressed the second part of the questionnaire containing questions related to the relevant part of the research on the impact of enablers of the fourth industrial revolution on processes in NPD project management. In addition, respondents provided answers in terms of project governance occurring in their organizations, which was ultimately used to determine the moderating effect of its enablers' impact on NPD project management.

Quantitative research was conducted using a questionnaire survey available on a specially designed database platform. In both the pre-test and the post-test, respondents completed a matrix, in which:

Information was collected (no personal data was collected as part of the research) on the company's sector of activity, headquarters (country), turnover, employment size, and type of projects carried out by the company; in addition,

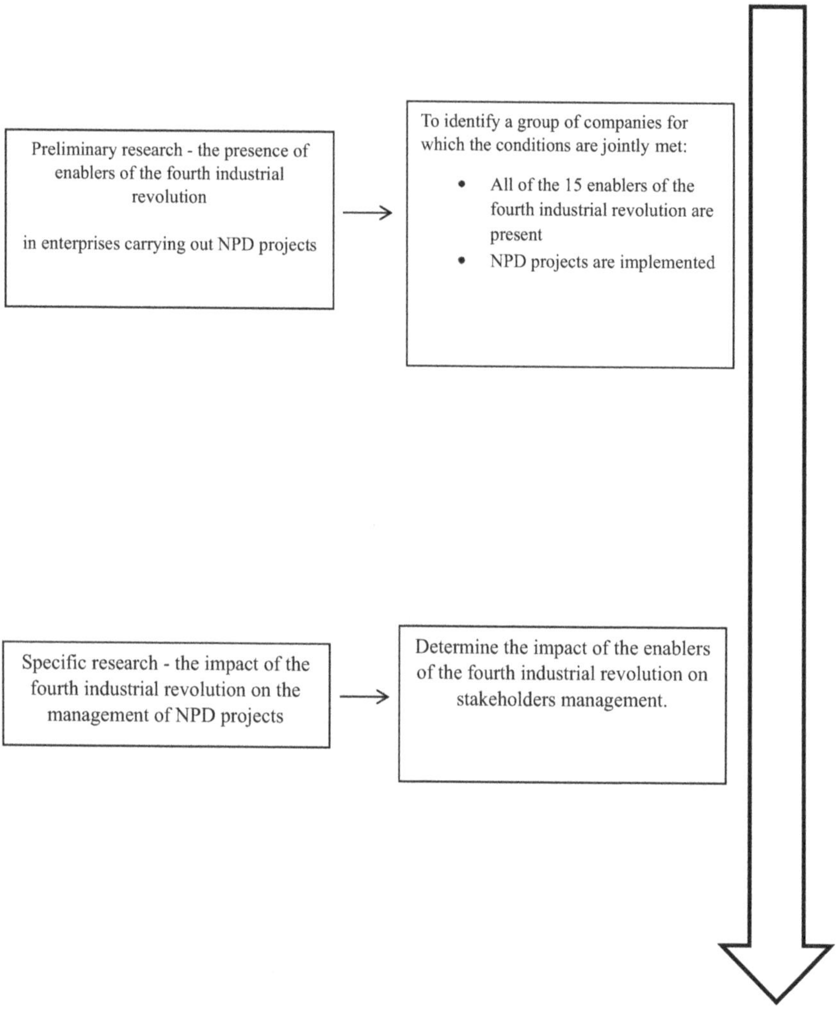

Figure 4.1 Adopted research model.

respondents indicated their role in projects and the number of years of experience in project activities.

The presence of enablers of the fourth industrial revolution in an enterprise was verified (enablers of the occurrence of the fourth industrial revolution were identified as a result of research. Arranged in Table 4.3 according to the frequency of occurrence in the analyzed scientific publications).

In the research proper, respondents determined the level of impact of each of the enablers of the fourth industrial revolution on individual processes in the management of the NPD project. The questionnaire used a seven-point Likert scale,

Table 4.3 Enablers of the fourth industrial revolution used in enterprise surveys

Identifier	*Enabler*
E1	Internet of Things (IoT)
E2	Cyber physical systems (CPS)
E3	Big data
E4	Cloud computing
E5	Additive manufacturing
E6	Autonomous robots
E7	Augmented reality
E8	Artificial intelligence
E9	Virtual reality (VR)
E10	Deep learning
E11	Automation
E12	Digital twins
E13	Simulation
E14	Data analytics
E15	Cyber security

ranging from −3 to +3, whereby individual negative values indicated a negative impact, positive values a positive impact and a zero value no impact. Thus, in the survey, the value +3 corresponded to a significant positive impact; +2—to a moderate positive impact; +1—to a low positive impact. The situation was analogous for negative impact.

Among the topic areas, stakeholders (ST) governance processes were highlighted.

As a result of the preliminary research, completed questionnaires were obtained from 1,152 enterprises. In accordance with the adopted criterion (the eligibility criterion adopted for the specific research assumed that all of the 15 previously identified enablers of the fourth industrial revolution were present in the firms and that the firms were conducting NPD projects) 438 enterprises from this group were selected for proper research. As a result of the undertaken activities, finally we received 372 correctly filled in, complete (duplicates, questionnaires that were not fully completed, and those in which there were obvious repetitions of the same answers regardless of the question asked, were deleted) questionnaires, which constituted a research sample qualified for further statistical analyses.

The respondents in the survey were mostly project managers (41%) and project team members (22%). The others were program manager (17%) and project portfolio manager (9%), and 11% of respondents had another project-related role.

The majority (42%) of respondents had 6–10 years of experience in project activities and 26% had 11–15 years. The shortest experience (1–5 years) was declared by 12% of respondents, and there were 11% of people in the 16–20 years range. The longest experience (over 20 years) was declared by 9% of respondents.

The respondents represented companies headquartered in 16 countries: The United States, Germany, Switzerland, Denmark, Sweden, Italy, Finland, Great Britain, France, India, Japan, South Korea, Poland, Austria, Slovenia, and Spain.

More than half of the surveyed companies (64%) had their headquarters in three countries, i.e., the United States, Germany, and Switzerland.

All of the participating companies conducted NPD project activities in the manufacturing sector. These were companies employing over 250 people with an annual turnover of over 20 million EUR.

The data analysis did not show any statistically significant correlation between the characteristics of the respondents (role in project activities, number of years of experience) and the country of the enterprise and the obtained research results.

Data analysis was performed using the IBM SPSS Statistics 25 software. In the presentation of the research findings in this monograph, selected issues from the full report of statistical (the full statistical data processing report was prepared by Maciej Wolny, PhD, Eng.: Wolny, M. "Statistical analysis summaries of survey data using SPSS software" [unpublished report]) analyses were used, elaborated, and subjected to inference, in accordance with the research narrative adopted.

To verify the reliability of the research tool used, the Cronbach's alpha coefficient (Peterson 1994) was calculated for each group of responses E1 – E15 (Table 4.4). As the lowest of the obtained results was 0.849, it should be concluded that the internal consistency of the tool was demonstrated, therefore the validity and reliability of the obtained data was confirmed.

Statistical analyses of data obtained as a result of the conducted research were made with the use of:

- Descriptive statistics in the form of frequency tables (mean, median, dominant, standard deviation, skewness, skewness standard error, kurtosis, kurtosis standard error, minimum, maximum, percentiles) and histograms;
- Factor analyses (scree plots, principal component matrices, resources of common variation, matrices of rotated principal components, total explained variances, matrices of transformed components);
- Regression analyses, correlation, ANOVA, residual statistics.

The test results were considered in terms of:

- Analysis of the impact of enablers of the fourth industrial revolution on individual thematic areas and stages in the project management cycle;
- Determining the way the design order impacts the impact of the enablers of the fourth industrial revolution on the processes in project management.

Table 4.4 Reliability statistics

Cronbach's alpha														
E1	*E2*	*E3*	*E4*	*E5*	*E6*	*E7*	*E8*	*E9*	*E10*	*E11*	*E12*	*E13*	*E14*	*E15*
.972	.926	.905	.917	.910	.896	.914	.923	.933	.920	.948	.879	.902	.849	.883

In the interpretation of the mean positive impact results, the following rating scale was adopted: [0≥0.5]—no effect; [0.5≥1.0]—very little impact; [1.0≥1.5]—low impact; [1.5≥2.0]—moderate impact; [2.0≥2.5]—high impact; [2.5–3.0]—significant impact. A similar scale was adopted for the negative impact.

Furthermore, the research identified a method for extracting the components of the fourth industrial revolution affecting either the process theme groups or the processes within the stages of the project management cycle. It consists in separating, in the course of the research procedure, groups (bundles) of enablers of the fourth industrial revolution according to the adopted criteria, which were defined for each thematic area in project management and for the stages of the project management cycle. These criteria are membership of the main component (determined by the principal components factor analysis conducted) as well as the strength and direction of impact (determined by the previously performed statistical analysis of the empirical data obtained from the conducted research) of a given enabler of the fourth industrial revolution.

The research procedure adopted a method of extracting key enablers of the fourth industrial revolution influencing thematic groups of processes or processes within the stages of the project management cycle. It consists in compiling the results of descriptive statistics analyses of the average strength of the impact of individual enablers of the fourth industrial revolution on a given area within the components identified during the research. As a result of this method, for each component, the key factor that had the greatest strength of impact (rounded to two decimal places) on a given area is identified. If more than one factor of the same strength occurs, they are all qualified as key.

Results related to the impact of fourth industrial revolution enablers on stakeholders' management

The research produced data to determine the impact of fourth industrial revolution enablers on stakeholders' management.

Analysis of the histograms in terms of the impact of the enablers of the fourth industrial revolution on stakeholders' management in the project revealed that further inferences can be made about the strength of the impact based on the mean values in this area, as the distributions in question are close to normal.

On the basis of the research performed, it was noted that the impact of individual factors varied (Table 4.5). At the same time, the analysis of the results leads to the conclusion that for factors E9 and E10 there are indications for further in-depth studies in the future regarding the aggregation of the influence of these assets in the area of stakeholders in project management.

In the course of the analysis of the results obtained, it can be concluded that there are six factors that have a strong impact on stakeholder management in the project. One factor (E1) has a moderate impact, one activator (E4) has a small impact on the area under consideration, very little impact is shown by factors E10 and E8, while the remaining factors (E5, E2, E11, E6) have no impact on stakeholder management in the project. The only factor with a negative (moderate) impact is E15.

Table 4.5 Descriptive statistics of the impact of fourth industrial revolution enablers on project stakeholders' management

Statistics		*E1_ST*	*E2_ST*	*E3_ST*	*E4_ST*	*E5_ST*	*E6_ST*
N	Valid	372	372	372	372	372	372
	Missing data	0	0	0	0	0	0
Average		1.7285	0.0202	2.1801	1.4140	0.0780	–0.0430
Median		1.5000	0.0000	2.5000	1.5000	0.0000	0.0000
Mode		1.50	0.00	2.50	1.50	0.00	0.00
Standard deviation		0.91495	0.54599	0.57093	0.67841	0.62783	0.53152
Skewness		–0.346	0.032	–0.466	–0.329	0.426	–0.044
Skewness standard error		0.126	0.126	0.126	0.126	0.126	0.126
Kurtosis		–0.676	–0.173	–0.314	–0.102	0.046	0.092
Standard kurtosis error		0.252	0.252	0.252	0.252	0.252	0.252
Minimum		–0.50	–1.00	0.50	–0.50	–1.00	–1.50
Maximum		3.00	1.00	3.00	3.00	1.50	1.00
Percentile	25	1.0000	0.0000	1.5000	1.0000	–0.5000	–0.3750
	50	1.5000	0.0000	2.5000	1.5000	0.0000	0.0000
	75	2.5000	0.5000	2.5000	2.0000	0.5000	0.0000

Statistics		*E7_ST*	*E8_ST*	*E9_ST*	*E10_ST*	*E11_ST*	*E12_ST*
N	Valid	372	372	372	372	372	372
	Missing data	0	0	0	0	0	0
Average		2.2164	0.5901	2.2137	0.6680	0.0013	2.3347
Median		2.5000	0.0000	2.5000	0.5000	0.0000	2.5000
Mode		2.50	0.00	2.50	0.00	0.00	2.50
Standard deviation		0.55996	1.22114	0.55859	1.14719	0.45186	0.46750
Skewness		–0.601	0.614	–0.552	0.558	0.656	–0.411

Skewness standard error		0.126	0.126	0.126	0.126	0.126	0.126
Kurtosis		0.023	–0.864	0.212	–0.850	5.802	–0.415
Standard kurtosis error		0.252	0.252	0.252	0.252	0.252	0.252
Minimum		0.50	–1.50	0.50	–1.00	–1.00	1.00
Maximum		3.00	3.00	3.00	3.00	3.00	3.00
Percentile	25	2.0000	–0.5000	2.0000	0.0000	0.0000	2.0000
	50	2.5000	0.0000	2.5000	0.5000	0.0000	2.5000
	75	2.5000	1.5000	2.5000	1.5000	0.0000	2.5000

Statistics		*E13_ST*	*E14_ST*	*E15_ST*
N	Valid	372	372	372
	Missing data	0	0	0
Average		2.4019	2.0228	–1.8965
Median		2.5000	2.0000	–2.0000
Mode		2.50	2.00	–2.00
Standard deviation		0.45902	0.50618	0.78696
Skewness		–0.463	–0.343	0.672
Skewness standard error		0.126	0.126	0.126
Kurtosis		–0.269	0.022	0.154
Standard kurtosis error		0.252	0.252	0.252
Minimum		1.00	0.00	–3.00
Maximum		3.00	3.00	0.50
Percentile	25	2.0000	1.5000	–2.5000
	50	2.5000	2.0000	–2.0000
	75	2.5000	2.5000	–1.5000

Table 4.6 Results of factor analysis of the main components of the impact of enablers of the fourth industrial revolution on the project stakeholders' management (Matrix of rotated components)

	Components				
	1	*2*	*3*	*4*	*5*
E10_ST	0.879	0.095	–0.022	–0.008	–0.048
E8_ST	0.870	0.215	0.049	0.020	–0.004
E14_ST	0.702	0.023	0.038	0.000	–0.014
E1_ST	0.697	0.414	0.064	0.014	0.035
E4_ST	0.046	0.663	–0.031	0.109	–0.093
E9_ST	–0.011	0.651	–0.053	–0.201	0.128
E3_ST	0.080	0.620	–0.118	0.090	0.006
E7_ST	0.180	0.618	0.138	0.233	–0.025
E15_ST	–0.354	–0.611	–0.073	–0.022	–0.128
E12_ST	0.139	0.522	0.130	–0.095	–0.080
E6_ST	–0.065	0.015	0.790	0.007	–0.227
E11_ST	–0.193	–0.025	–0.538	0.027	–0.426
E5_ST	–0.194	0.022	–0.290	0.721	–0.098
E13_ST	0.218	0.070	0.307	0.702	0.135
E2_ST	–0.096	–0.015	–0.112	0.022	0.871

Notes
Method of extracting factors—main components.
[a] Rotation method used was Varimax with Kaiser normalization and the rotation converged in 10 iterations

Based on the factor analysis of the obtained results of the conducted research, five main components affecting stakeholder management in the project were identified (Table 4.6.). While it was observed that the first component includes E10, E8, E14, E1, the second, more numerous components are E4, E9, E3, E7, E15, E12, the third main component is E6 and E11, and the fourth is E5 and E13. A separate component, however, is E2.

Main contributions

In the area of stakeholders, a negative correlation of E15 was observed with the other factors of the relevant principal component, which, with the previous observation of the moderate strength of the influence of factor E15 on stakeholder management in the project, is worth noting for further consideration. It should be mentioned that factor E11 also showed a negative correlation, but was previously classified as having no impact on stakeholder management in the project, and therefore the negative orientation of its correlation is not significant for further inference.

Thus, as a result of the inference made from the statistical analyses on the basis of the principal components, it was decided to identify the components of the fourth industrial revolution according to the previously adopted criteria of strength and direction of influence:

- Component 1 with factors having a positive impact on stakeholder management in the project: deep learning, artificial intelligence (AI), data analytics, IoT;
- Component 2 with factors having a positive impact on stakeholder management in the project: cloud computing, virtual reality (VR), big data, augmented reality, digital representation of objects (digital twins);
- Component 3 with factors that have a positive impact on stakeholder management in the project: simulations;
- Component 4 with factors having a negative impact on the area and stakeholders in project management: cyber security.

As a result of the research undertaken, the following key activators of the fourth industrial revolution for stakeholder management in the project were identified using the author's method adopted:

- data analytics,
- digital representation of objects (digital twins),
- simulations,
- cyber security.

It should be noted that the first three of the key activators have a strong positive impact, while cyber security negatively affects (moderately) integration management in the project.

The bottom line is that when managing projects in a sustainable manner and using an agile approach, we should pay special attention to stakeholder management. With the rise of Industry 4.0, our attentions should be particularly applied to issues related to data analysis, the concept of digital twins, and simulations, as these aspects can support sustainable and agile project management. In addition, our efforts should also be crowned on the right approach to cyber security, as this factor can hinder the development of sustainable and agile project management.

References

André, J.C. (2019). *Industry 4.0:* Paradoxes and Conflicts: Wiley.

Chen, Y.B. (2017). Integrated and intelligent manufacturing: perspectives and enablers. *Engineering, 3* (5), pp. 588–595.

Faul, A., Jazdi, N., Weyrich, M. (2016). *Approach to interconnect existing industrial automation systems with the industrial internet.* Paper presented at the 21st IEEE International Conference on Emerging Technologies and Factory Automation (ETFA), OWL University of Applied Science, Fraunhofer IOSB-INA, Berlin, Germany.

Ganzarain, J., Errasti, N. (2016). Three stage maturity model in SME's towards Industry 4.0. *Journal of Industrial Engineering and Management-Jiem, 9* (5), pp. 1119–1128.

Kagermann, H., Lukas, W.-D., Wahlster, W. (2011). Industrie 4.0: Mit dem Internet der Dinge auf dem Weg zur 4. industriellen Revolution. VDI Nachrichten, p. 2.

Liao, Y.X., Deschamps, F., Loures, E.D.R., Ramos, L.F.P. (2017). Past, present and future of Industry 4.0 — a systematic literature review and research agenda proposal. *International Journal of Production Research, 55* (12), pp. 3609–3629

Moeuf, A., Lamouri, S., Pellerin, R., Tamayo-Giraldo, S., Tobon-Valencia, E., Eburdy, R. (2019). Identification of critical success factors, risks and opportunities of Industry 4.0 in SMEs. *International Journal of Production Research,* 58 (5), pp. 1384–1400.
Pacchini, A.P.T., Lucato, W.C., Facchini, F., Mummolo, G. (2019). The degree of readiness for the implementation of Industry 4.0. *Computers in Industry, 113*, pp. 103–125.
Peterson, R. A. (1994). A meta-analysis of cronbach's coefficient alpha. *Journal of Consumer Research, 21*, 381–391. http://dx.doi.org/10.1086/209405
Qin, J., Liu, Y., Grosvenor, R. (2016). A categorical framework of manufacturing for Industry 4.0 and beyond. *Sixth International Conference on Changeable, Agile, Reconfigurable and Virtual Production (Carv2016), 52*, pp. 173–178.
Rüßmann, M., Lorenz, M., Gerbert, P., Waldner, M., Justus, J., Engel, P., et al. (2015). Industry 4.0: the future of productivity and growth in manufacturing industries. *Boston Consulting Group, 9* (1), pp. 54–89.
Sanders, A., Elangeswaran, C., Wulfsberg, J. (2016). Industry 4.0 implies lean manufacturing: research activities in Industry 4.0 function as enablers for lean manufacturing. *Journal of Industrial Engineering and Management-Jiem, 9* (3), pp. 811–833.
Wang, Q., Shang, J.W. (2023). Analysis of the quality improvement path of supply chain management under the background of Industry 4.0. *International Journal of Technology Management*, *91*(1-2), 1–18.

5 Sustainable project management in nonprofit organizations

Research results from Poland

Anna Marciszewska, Renata Brajer-Marczak and Anna Zabłocka-Kluczka

The specifics of the nonprofit organizations functioning

The activity and impact of nonprofit organizations (NPOs) is constantly increasing worldwide (Liceran-Gutierrez et al., 2022; Saidoun, 2020; Casey, 2016; Colás, 2013; Salamon, 2010; Salamon and Sokolowski, 2016). NPOs are complex entities, distinguished by their ability to work for specific groups. Thanks to characteristics such as flexibility of action and social commitment, these organizations have developed effective methods of working for the benefit of different groups of service recipients. What distinguishes NPOs from businesses is that financial resources are a means to an end, rather than the objective of the activities undertaken. The effectiveness of an NPO is seen through the prism of activities aimed at both the objectives pursued and the rational management of resources. It becomes important to define the right objectives for action, which should be derived from the actual needs of potential service recipients (rather than the needs of the organization), taking into account their scale and hierarchy (Jałocha and Bogacz-Wojtanowska, 2017). In addition, NPOs, compared to businesses, base their activities very much on shared values and a strong motivation to contribute to their environment, which is very diverse and linked to different fundraising sources.

NPOs are important actors in multi- and cross-sectoral ecosystems. The scope of their activities involves reaching out to the most vulnerable groups in society in need of support. These organizations have a significant impact on both the social and natural environment. They are presented as institutions of civil society that encourage interaction around a common goal, giving these initiatives a formal character. The rationale for their establishment most often has to do with the inadequacies of market mechanisms and the need to support them, not as a full replacement but, rather, as a supplement. In these organizations, in addition to full-time employees, there are also volunteers who offer their time without a salary because they identify with the organization's aims and values. There is a high turnover among volunteers, so motivating them and keeping them engaged throughout the project is a challenge for leaders (Seiler and Bortnowska, 2020). The difference in influence among staff, volunteers and founders distinguishes NPOs from business entities and indicates greater democratic processes in place for decision-making (Domański, 2012).

DOI: 10.4324/9781003356059-6

At the same time it can be seen that in NPOs globally, regardless of their nature a widely used practice is project management (Golini et al., 2015). In Poland, many NPOs carry out large-scale projects and contribute to developing a strong and credible third sector (Jałocha and Bogacz-Wojtanowska, 2017). The projects implemented by NPOs contribute to the solution of many complex socio-economic and environmental problems. Through effective project management, these entities can significantly improve their organization and increase the effectiveness of their actions yielding environmental benefits at the same time. This creates a growing expectation to apply a sustainable approach to project management. In order to meet this, it is useful to discern the project management methodologies used by NPOs.

The concept of sustainable project management fits very much into NPOs. The need to relate this issue to NPOs stems from the increase in the share and importance of projects, and the diversity and breadth of consequences of project implementation in these organizations (Trocki, 2020). The nature of NPOs can be described as mission-driven, meaning that they aim to change social reality in accordance with shared values.

Sustainable project management in nonprofit organizations

Today, in NPOs, projects may provide a solution to many complex socio-economic and environmental problems. Sustainable project management involves planning, monitoring and controlling the implementation and support processes of projects, taking into account environmental, social and economic aspects. It should address the project life cycle, the processes involved in projects, and the results and outcomes achieved. It is oriented toward stakeholder benefits and the implementation of projects in a transparent, fair and ethical manner that includes the active participation of different stakeholders (Silvius and Schipper, 2010, p. 6). This means adopting a different, more holistic perspective of project implementation that takes into account, in addition to the classic parameters (time, cost, scope), new factors such as benefits, values, risks and sustainable effects for different stakeholders (Trocki et al., 2020). In this way, there is a shift in the scope of project management from the traditional management of time, budget and quality toward the management of social, environmental and economic impacts (Silvius and Schipper, 2014, p. 80).

In September 2015, world leaders adopted the UN program "Transforming our World: the 2030 Agenda for Sustainable Development" and the Sustainable Development Goals. The adoption of the Agenda forms the basis of a new paradigm focused on addressing economic, social and environmental disparities in a universal and integrated manner (European Economic and Social Committee, 2022). At the micro level, this agenda relates to the activities of individual organizations. Organizational sustainability is based on the so-called Triple Bottom Line (TBL) model. The model illustrates the equivalence of three spheres/developmental lines, referred to as the Triple P: People, Planet and Profit/Prosperity. According to this concept, sustainable development is in harmony with economic and social stability, and environmental sustainability (Elkington and Rowlands, 1999). The importance of this research area stems from the growing relevance of projects in the economy and the activities of individual organizations. Projects are becoming the source of a variety of development benefits, as well as for risks and negative impacts (Nieto-Rodrigez, 2012; Schoper et al., 2018).

Therefore, more interest in this topic can be expected in the near future. This is confirmed by studies reported in the literature (Wawak and Wozniak, 2020) indicating that sustainable project management is one of three new and growing trends in project management publications. Therefore, it seems inevitable to undertake research aimed at providing answers to the question of whether it is possible to implement this approach in NPOs as well. The issue of sustainability and social responsibility of the project activities of NPOs is an emerging research area. Undertaking research in this area is important both from the perspective of organizational and project management, and social needs (Corboni et al., 2020). The goals set by NPOs correspond with the 17 Sustainable Development Goals that were adopted in the aforementioned resolution (Transforming our World, 2015). The UN, together with business leaders, governments and the scientific community, jointly endorsed these goals, recognizing them as the best way to address the sustainability challenges that NPOs also face (Corboni et al., 2020, p. 22). These goals cover areas such as fighting poverty, combating hunger, climate change, economic inequality, sustainable consumption, pursuing peace, justice, reducing social inequality and promoting strong, sustainable, inclusive economic development, among others. These goals are interrelated so that the achievement of one contributes to the success of the others.

The challenges of today's world mean that every company, institution or NPO should strive to develop appropriate policies and practices that allow development without negative consequences for society and the environment. This is one of the most important challenges of modern organizations and, in particular, corresponds to the specifics of NPOs whose social activities (e.g., fighting poverty, discrimination, lack of access to education) are carried out through projects aimed at the above problem areas. Currently, considerations of sustainable project management refer primarily to business organizations, but it seems inevitable to adapt this approach also in projects implemented by NPOs (Saidoun, 2020; Subedi and Wagner, 2018).

The arguments for undertaking research in the area of sustainable project management in NPOs are: (1) the perception of NPOs as project organizations; (2) the specifics of the projects implemented (complexity, uniqueness, stakeholders); and (3) the growing importance of projects as instruments of change. At the same time, given the difference between NPOs and business organizations, the question arises whether the frequency with which the sustainable project management practices are exercised in NPOs will be significantly different from the frequency of exercised practices in the aforementioned area in the case of business organizations. There is at least a few sustainability-based project management standards. In this work the standard of the Global Alliance for Project Professions (GAPPS) and the International Competence Baseline v 3.0 (IPMA methodology), called Green Project Management (GPM) and studied in terms of the three pillars: People,

Planet and Prosperity, was taken. It can be assumed that with regard to environmental and prosperity-related solutions in sustainable project management, NPOs may perform worse than business organizations. To the contrary, in the social sphere, there is no reason to assume that the frequency with which the sustainable project management practices are exercised in NPOs is significantly different from that of business organizations. In the context of the above, the following research hypothesis was adopted:

> H1: *The frequency with which the sustainable project management practices (GPM Practices) are exercised in nonprofit organizations (NPOs) is different from the frequency with which the sustainable project management practices are exercised in business entities.*

And – as the GPM is discussed in terms of the three pillars: People, Planet and Prosperity – three more specific hypotheses were adopted alongside:

> *H1a: The frequency with which the sustainable project management practices (GPM Practices) are exercised in the People area of nonprofit organizations (NPOs) is different than in business entities.*
>
> *H1b: The frequency with which the sustainable project management practices (GPM Practices) are exercised in the Planet area of nonprofit organizations (NPOs) is different than in business entities.*
>
> *H1c: The frequency with which the sustainable project management practices (GPM Practices) are exercised in the Prosperity area of nonprofit organizations (NPOs) is different than in business entities.*

Green Project Management vs project management methodologies

The sustainability-based project management promoted by GPM Global is based on the standards of the Global Alliance for Project Professions (GAPPS) and the International Competence Baseline v 3.0 (IPMA methodology). These are standards focused on integrating projects with the organization's strategy for sustainable development. One of the basic standards is the 5P standard (Standard for Sustainability in Project Management: People, Planet, Prosperity, Project, Processes and Products). It addresses the integration of projects into an organizational strategy for sustainability. It takes into account the ten principles of the UN Global Compact and GRI G4 and is based on the findings of ISO 21500. The standard consists of three domains: People (focusing on ethical performance and maintaining mutually beneficial relationships with employees, customers and the community), Planet (consists of areas such as transportation, energy, water, consumption) and Prosperity (addresses return on investment, business flexibility and economic prosperity and simulation). This standard represents, structures and defines the phenomena and concepts of sustainability in the field of project management (GPM Global, 2014). The adopted standards identify areas of sustainability, problems that occur in the various phases of the project life cycle and solutions that eliminate or reduce negative social, environmental and economic impacts in all types of projects. They allow application to existing project management methodologies (Prince, TenStep, DSDM Agile). Indeed, it seems that these methodologies can influence sustainable project management.

GPM is studied in terms of the three pillars: People, Planet and Prosperity – Triple Bottom Line (Corboni et al., 2020). It is, therefore, important to recognize all the processes that make up these areas and identify the organization's strengths and weaknesses in project management. These areas, however, are not separate so that a prerequisite for achieving a sustainable level of project management is to achieve harmony between them. There are different classifications of project management methodologies.

Taking into account the manner of proceeding in the project management process one can distinguish between the sequentially driven (waterfall, traditional) and iterative (agile) project management methodologies. The traditional approach to project management emphasizes the need to define objectives and solutions. This means a clear and precise definition of requirements, little change in the scope of the project, and the use of established and proven templates for proceeding. Advantages include a defined plan for the entire project, known resource requirements and the lack of need for a top-performing team. Conversely, weaknesses include little ability to make changes to the project plan, the need for detailed plans, an excessive level of project formalization, the risk of high costs and project protraction, and lack of focus on the real needs of the client and the value delivered (Alleman, 2005).

Agile methodologies are based on a distinctive approach of "team manager–project team members" relationship. In this case, the project manager acts as a coach and mentor (Zakrzewska et al., 2022). This translates into the development of self-organizing teams. Research confirms that project stakeholder satisfaction, appropriate project team competences, personal development of team members and a high level of communication are responsible for project effectiveness (Shenhar and Dvir, 2007). These attributes of Agile can be combined with the development lines indicated in the TBL model (e.g., in response to stakeholder needs, the negative environmental impact of the product can be reduced). The Agile methodology is recommended for projects where the role of managers is crucial, as sensitive issues such as cost and effort require constant monitoring and attention. It is now used regardless of the size, sector or business environment in which an organization operates (Whitelock, 2019; Nagaria et al., 2019). Also evident in the Agile approach is the consideration of stakeholder needs and expectations throughout the project life cycle (Zakrzewska et al., 2022; Gareis et al., 2011), and this is important in GPM. A characteristic of Agile is an orientation to long-term benefits (Sońta-Drączkowska and Mrożewski, 2020), which also corresponds to the assumptions of GPM and concerns for access to resources by future generations. Table 5.1 indicates the characteristics of each approach in project management.

Project management methodologies are a key component of the project environment in organizations. They are the primary source of project knowledge in all phases of a project. They act as standards and procedures describing the activities and processes necessary to achieve project success. In view of the wealth

Table 5.1 Sustainability and project management methodologies

Assumptions of sustainability	*Characteristics of the traditional project management*	*Characteristics of the Agile project management*
Long-term orientation	Short-term orientation	Short and long-term orientation
Consideration of the interest of today and future generation	Consideration of the interest of sponsor/stakeholders	Consideration of the interest of all project stakeholders (including project team members)
Value-orientation	Deliverable/results-orientation/speed to market-orientation	Value-orientation/speed to value-orientation
Focus on: people, planet, profit	Focus on: fixed scope, various time and budget	Focus on: fixed time and cost, various scope
Consideration of increasing complexity	Reduction of complexity	Giving answer to increasing complexity

Source: Zakrzewska et al. (2022, p.5).

of methodological support for project management, it is impossible to indicate unequivocally which methodology is closer to sustainable project management. On the one hand, comparing assumptions of sustainability and characteristics of discussed project management methodologies presented in Table 5.1, agile methodology seems to be closer, on the other hand – GPM is based on the traditional approach to project management. Therefore, it seems interesting to check whether any of them affects the higher frequency of application of the GPM practices in the NPOs. Considering the above, the following research hypothesis was formulated:

> H2a–c: *There is a positive relationship between Project management methodology and the frequency with which the sustainable project management practices (GPM Practices) in general and in particular areas ((a)People, (b) Planet, (c) Prosperity) are exercised in nonprofit organizations (NPOs).*

Purpose of the research and description of the research process

The research process was planned and carried out in four main stages: (1) critical analysis of the literature on the subject; (2) preparation of the research; (3) quantitative research; and (4) analysis of the research results and conclusion. Each stage was a logical continuation of the stages carried out previously. The research has been performed in the scope of the project financed by the Ministry of Science and Higher Education in Poland under the program "Regional Initiative of Excellence" 2019–2022 project number 015/RID/2018/19 total funding amount 1,072,104,000 PLN.

The critical analysis of the literature enabled the conceptual framework for the quantitative study to be defined. The identified research gap – the lack of studies dedicated to GPM in NPOs in the literature (Kloppenborg and Opfer, 2002; Khang

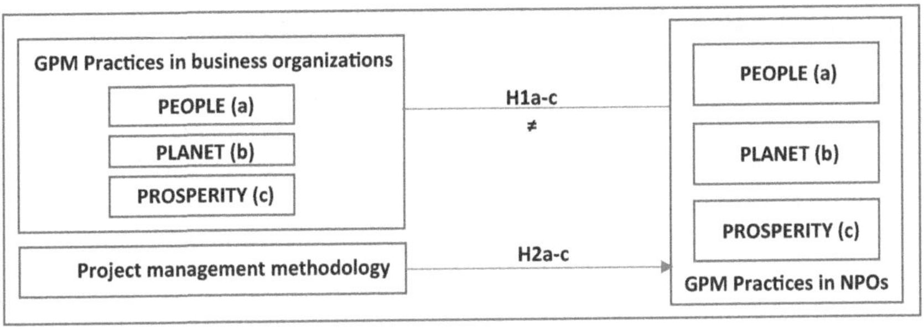

Figure 5.1 Research model.

Source: Own study.

and Moe, 2008; Patrizia and Massimo, 2014; Waters and Ott, 2014; Golini et al., 2015) – allowed us to adopt the perspective of NPOs and to formulate the main objective of the research, i.e. to identify the frequency with which the GPM practices are exercised in NPOs in Poland alongside the following specific objectives:

- verification of whether the frequency of application of the GPM practices significantly differs in NPOs and in business organizations;
- verification of whether application of specific project management methodologies fosters more frequent applications of GPM practices in the NPOs.

In the present investigation, the dependent variable was the frequency of sustainable project management practices exercised in NPOs (*GPM Practices*), which consisted of three dimensions: People, Planet and Prosperity. The research used a modified questionnaire to assess the frequency of sustainable project management in NPOs. The questionnaire was based on the P5 Global Project Management standard and the research of Juchniewicz (2019), who proposed a tool to measure the social responsibility of project activities in business. Figure 5.1 presents the adopted research model and the developed research hypotheses.

Variable measurement

In order to examine the proposed hypotheses, three key variables were defined: Project Management Methodology (*PMM*), the frequency of application of the Green Project Management Practices (*GPM Practices*) with supporting variables: People, Planet and Prosperity. *PMM* describes how the projects were implemented in organizations, and was built as a two-value variable: 1 – traditional (waterfall) methodology; and 2 – Agile methodology.

Green Project Management Practices (*GPM Practices*) is a variable designed to evaluate the frequency of application of the GPM. Items constituting the variable and the scale, on which they were assessed, were taken from the literature

(Juchniewicz, 2019, pp. 181–187) and adapted to NPOs. Respondents answered using a point scale with the following options to choose from: 0 – I don't know, 1 – never or in a few projects implemented in the organization, 2 – usually/in most projects implemented in the organization, 3 – always/in each project implemented in the organization, 9 – not applicable. The *GPM Practices* variable is built using a 3-point scale (never, usually, always) as a mean of three auxiliary variables: People, Planet and Prosperity.

In order to build the *People* variable, 39 items assigned into 14 groups were used. Items were rated on the previously described 3-point scale (never, usually, always).

In order to build the *Planet* variable 12 items were assigned. The used items described the organization's environmental activities aimed at minimizing transport costs or use of environmentally friendly means of transport, reducing energy costs and resource consumption during the implementation of projects. They were rated on the same 3-point scale.

The *Prosperity* variable was measured using five items describing benefits from the implemented projects, here, again, the 3-point scale was used.

Data gathering process and characteristics of the research sample

In order to verify the proposed hypotheses and identify the frequency of application of the GPM practices in the NPOs and those factors that may affect it, a questionnaire study was devised. The survey was conducted using the CAWI (Computer-Assisted Web Interview) method, which allowed information to be obtained at low cost and provided a short turnaround time. A research platform was used in the data collection process, which enabled the e-form to be completed online. The respondents were NPOs in Poland. The research was focused on a combination of two topics: GPM and methodologies used in project management.

The research process was carried out in two stages, between January and February 2023. Purposeful sampling was used. In the first part, an invitation to participate in the survey was sent to publicly available e-mail addresses of foundations and associations operating in Poland that met the conditions of the project experience. The invitation to participate in the survey was sent to 684 organizations. Twenty-two completed questionnaires were received. The survey return rate was therefore 3.2%. In the second stage – using the LinkedIn Sales Navigator tool – project managers, project coordinators, project leaders and people managing projects and performing any one of these functions in NPOs operating in Poland were reached directly with an invitation to participate in the survey. The list covered 94 organizations. Eighteen questionnaires were received in return. In this case, the return rate was much higher at 19.15%. Finally, the survey was conducted on a group of 40 NPOs and the total return rate of the questionnaires was 5.14%.

The questionnaire was addressed to and completed by people who have the widest possible knowledge of project management in NPOs (62.5% members of NPO boards, 22.5% persons acting as project coordinators/managers, and 15%

Table 5.2 Research sample characteristics

		Registered association [N]	*Foundation [n]*	*Sum [N]*	*Sum [%]*
Public Benefit Organization (PBO)[a]	Yes	13	11	24	60.0
	No	6	10	16	40.0
Business area (serving market)	Local	7	2	9	22.5
	Regional	7	6	13	32.5
	Domestic	4	12	16	40.0
	International	1	1	2	5.0
NPOs' age	Up to 5 years	1	4	5	12.5
	6–10 years	1	3	4	10.0
	11–15 years	3	3	6	15.0
	16–20 years	4	3	7	17.5
	Over 20 years	10	8	18	45.0
NPOs' size[b]	Micro	5	6	11	27.5
	Small	1	6	7	17.5
	Medium	2	4	6	15.0
	Large	0	1	1	2.5
	Lack of data	11	4	15	35.5
Project management methodology	Traditional (waterfall)	17	16	33	82.5
	Agile	2	5	7	17.5

Source: Own research.

Notes

[a] Public Benefit Organizations – a term introduced in Poland on 1 January 2004 by the provisions of the Public Benefit Activity and Volunteerism Act. Having the status of a PBO is connected with certain privileges (e.g., the possibility of receiving 1.5 % tax from individuals), and obligations (e.g., the necessity to introduce more demanding self-control mechanisms inside the organization, transparency of activities and finances).

[b] The size of the NPO determined on the basis of the number of employees employed under an employment contract and standard criteria for classifying organizations in terms of size: micro (0–9), small (<10–49), medium (<50–249), large (250 people and more).

other members of the organization). Detailed information on the surveyed NPOs is presented in Table 5.2.

The majority of the surveyed organizations ran projects using the traditional (waterfall) methods (82.5%), while only 17.5% used the Agile methodology. None of the surveyed organizations had a certificate related to competences in the field of sustainable development and social responsibility. There are almost as many registered associations (47.5%) as foundations (52.5%) in the sample. Sixty percent of them were Public Benefit Organizations. The vast majority of the surveyed NPOs were experienced organizations: 45% of them have been operating on the market for over 20 years, 32.5% for at least ten years (between ten to 20 years) and only 22.5% have been on the market for less than ten years. They were operating mainly on domestic (40%), regional (32.5%) or local (22.5%) markets rarely venturing outside the borders of Poland. It seems that registered associations operate on the local market, while foundations on the domestic one. The results of the Chi-square ($\chi^2(3, N = 40)=6.772$; $p = 0.08$) and V-Cramer ($V = 0.411$; $p = 0.08$) tests, however, did not confirm this relationship in the tested sample.

The surveyed NPOs are involved in various types of activities: almost a quarter of them (22.5%) is involved in activities related to education and upbringing, the same number of surveyed organizations deals with social services and social assistance, 17.5% is involved with health protection, and 10% with the professional activation of the unemployed and the development of the labor market. Other types of activity are represented sporadically (e.g., only one of the surveyed organizations was involved in environmental protection).

The most popular sources of financing for the surveyed NPOs were donations from individuals (45.0%) and revenues from the transfer of 1% tax (42.5%). Next came proceeds from state (35.0%) and local government (35.0%) sources and donations from institutions (35.0%). The fourth most popular source was European Union structural funds (32.5%). The share of other sources of financing was significantly smaller.

Descriptive statistics and reliability analysis of scales

At the beginning of the research process, descriptive statistics and analysis of the internal consistency of response for tested variables were conducted. Cronbach's coefficient (α) was computed to test the reliability and internal consistency of the responses. The calculations were made using the PS Imago Pro ver. 7.0. For all tested variables, the Cronbach's α was acceptable (over 0.7) or high (over 0.8), which indicates a high internal reliability of the scales and measurements. As a next step, the normality of variable distribution was tested. For all tested variables, the standard error of kurtosis fits in the range <–2.2>. For variables *GPM Practices*, *Planet* and *Prosperity*, the standard error of skewness fits in the range <–2.2>, whereas for variable *People* it equals –2.16, which means that this variable distribution is close to normal, although slightly negatively skewed. For the rest of the examined variables, there are no grounds to reject the assumption of normality, which means that we can assume that variable distributions are normal. The results of this analysis are presented in Table 5.3.

Table 5.3 Defined variables along with the results of the reliability analysis of scales

No.	*Variable*	*No. of scales*	*Alfa-Cronbach*	*% var*	*M*	*SD*	*Skewness*	*Kurtosis*
1	*GPM Practices*	3	0.768	70.14	2.313	0.412	0.020	–0.553
1a	*People*	14	0.922	81.75	2.473	0.355	–0.809	0.563
1b	*Planet*	3	0.829	75.99	2.184	0.481	–0.016	–0.351
1c	*Prosperity*	5	0.833	69.75	2.207	0.569	–0.284	–0.580

Source: Own research.

The frequency of application of the Green Project Management Practices in surveyed NPOs

The overall frequency of application of the sustainable project management practices in the surveyed NPOs was counted as a mean of results obtained in three areas: *People*, *Planet* and *Prosperity* derived from the GPM P5 Model. Analysis of correlations between auxiliary variables showed that they are significantly statistically correlated (Table 5.4) and explain 70.14% of the variance of the *GPM Practices* variable.

In a 3-point scale, the frequency with which the GPM practices are exercised in the surveyed NPOs was rated at 2.313, which means that, usually, in most projects implemented in NPOs sustainable solutions are applied. Interestingly, there is a large discrepancy between assessments in particular areas. The *People* area was rated the best, *Planet* was rated the lowest and *Prosperity* did not fare much better (Figure 5.2).

The relatively high frequency of application of GPM practices in the *People* area results from the fact that they are often enforced by legal provisions (e.g. Labor Code, Data Protection Act) or requirements of project funders (EU Directives). The assessments in this area, however, are not homogeneous. The *People* variable was built from 14 auxiliary variables. Originally, in the questionnaire, two additional dimensions were adopted (*Obligation or compulsion to work* and *Bribery*). Due to the fact that it was not possible to build reliable scales for them, they were excluded from further study. They are, nevertheless, interesting at least for two reasons: first, their assessment differs significantly from the assessment of other variables and, second, these were the variables that the respondents had the greatest difficulty in evaluating, which is indicated by the percentage of "I do not know" or "It does not apply" answers (on average, this was indicated by approximately 50% of respondents and, in an extreme case, 72.5% of such answers were obtained in one of the questions). At the same time, extreme answers were very often indicated here. For this reason, they are presented in Figure 5.3 together with the other auxiliary variables included in the *People* variable.

Table 5.4 Correlation analysis between main auxiliary variables – *People, Planet, Prosperity*

Variables		*People*	*Planet*
Planet	*r*	0.501	
	p	0.001	
	N	38	
Prosperity	*r*	0.630	0.569
	p	<0.001	<0.001
	N	37	36

Source: Own research.

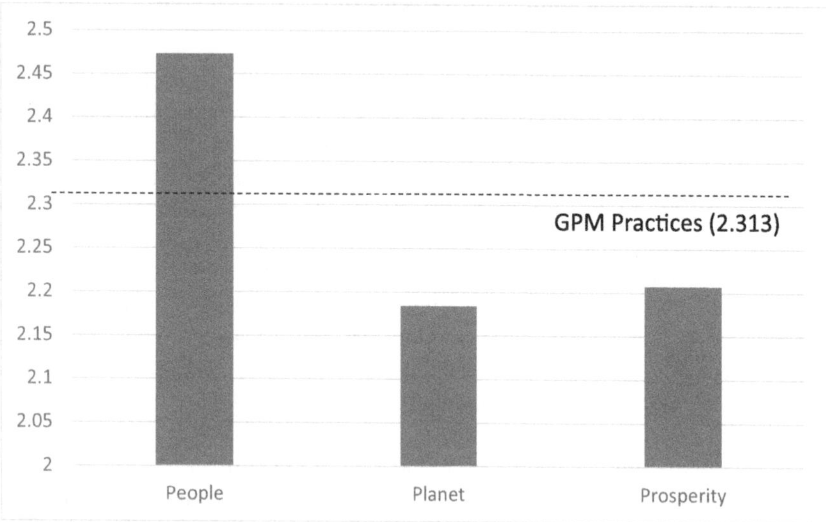

Figure 5.2 The frequency of application of the sustainable project management practices in surveyed NPOs.

Source: Own research.

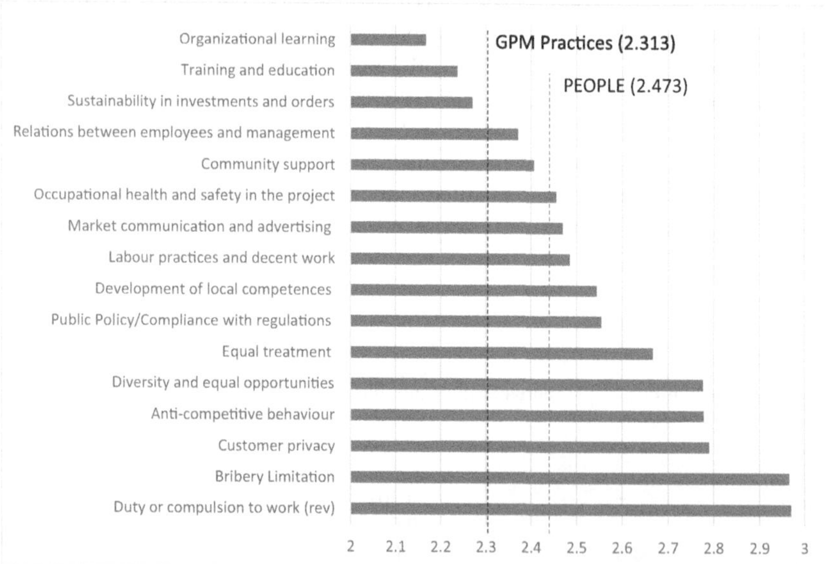

Figure 5.3 The assessment of the frequency with which the Green Project Management practices are exercised – auxiliary variables (PEOPLE).

Source: Own research.

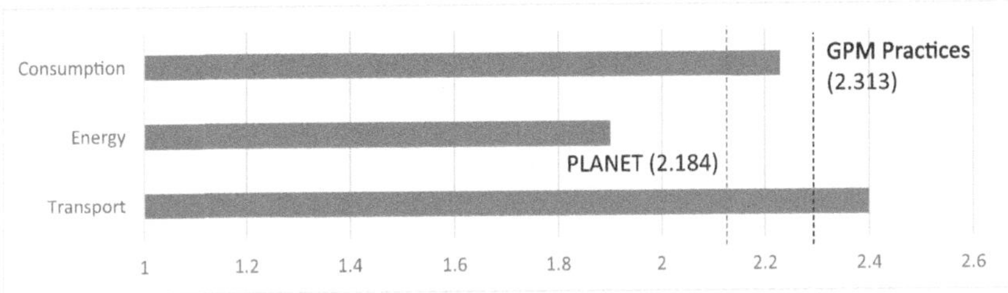

Figure 5.4 The assessment of the frequency with which the Green Project Management practices are exercised – auxiliary variables (PLANET).

Source: Own research.

Of the three areas, in which the frequency of application of GPM practices in NPOs was assessed, the *Planet* area was rated the lowest. The assessment of auxiliary variables built in this area is presented in Figure 5.4.

The frequency of application of GPM practices in NPOs and business organizations

In order to verify whether the frequency of application of GPM practices in NPOs and business organizations is similar or different, the Student's *t*-test for one trial was used. The results of GPM studies for business organizations conducted by Trocki and Juchniewicz (2017) and Trocki, Juchniewicz and Bukłaha (2020) according to the same model were taken as the reference point. The obtained results are presented in Table 5.5.

Analysis with the Student's *t*-test showed that in the surveyed sample, the overall frequency of application of GPM practices in NPOs is higher than in business organizations and this is a statistically significant difference. Thus, Hypothesis H1 can be accepted. There are some differences, however, between the components that have built this variable. The frequency of application of GPM practices in the *People* and *Prosperity* areas in NPOs is not statistically significantly different from the results obtained for business organizations, which means that both hypotheses H1a and H1c must be rejected. The obtained results show that respondents in NPOs assessed statistically significantly higher the frequency of application of GPM practices in the *Planet* area, than respondents in business organizations. This means that the H1b hypothesis can be accepted. It is also worth noting, that the tendency in the general level of assessment of particular areas (People, Planet, Prosperity) in NPOs is the same as in the case of business organizations, which is presented in Figure 5.5.

Analysis with the Student's *t*-test showed that in the surveyed sample, the frequency of application of GPM practices in the *People* area is the same in business and NPOs; however, there are some differences between the components that have

Table 5.5 The frequency of application of GPM practices in NPOs and business organizations – means comparison

No.	*Variable*	*M business org.*	*M NPOs*	*Test results*	*Result evaluation*
	GPM Practices	2.18	2.313	$t(39) = 2.039; p = 0.048$	Higher in NPOs
1	*People*	2.50	2.473	$t(39) = -0.483; p = 0.632$	Equal
2	*Planet*	1.89	2.184	$t(37) = 3.774; p < 0.001$	Higher in NPOs
3	*Prosperity*	2.14	2.207	$t(36) = 0.713; p = 0.480$	Equal
	Auxiliary variables (for *People*)				
1.1	Duty or compulsion to work (rev)	2.12	2.970	$t(32) = 28.040; p < 0.001$	Higher in NPOs
1.2	Bribery limitation	2.66	2.966	$t(28) = 8.860; p < 0.001$	Higher in NPOs
1.3	Customer privacy	2.84	2.790	$t(37) = -0.754; p = 0.456$	Equal
1.4	Anti-corruption behavior	2.63	2.778	$t(17) = 1.600; p = 0.128$	Equal
1.5	Diversity and equal opportunities	2.65	2.776	$t(37) = 2.151; p = 0.038$	Higher in NPOs
1.6	Equal treatment	2.69	2.667	$t(38) = -0.324; p = 0.747$	Equal
1.7	Public policy/Compliance with regulations	2.63	2.554	$t(36) = -1.158; p = 0.254$	Equal
1.8	Development of local competences	2.48	2.544	$t(37) = 0.866; p = 0.392$	Equal
1.9	Labor practices and decent work	2.70	2.485	$t(39) = -2.692; p = 0.010$	Lower in NPOs
1.10	Market communication and advertising	2.41	2.469	$t(31)=0.586; p = 0.562$	Equal
1.11	Occupational health and safety in the project	2.76	2.455	$t(36)=-3.194; p = 0.003$	Lower in NPOs
1.12	Community support	2.10	2.406	$t(38)=4.043; p <0.001$	Higher in NPOs
1.13	Relations between employees and management	2.48	2.371	$t(38)=-1.383; p = 0.175$	Equal
1.14	Sustainability in investments and orders	2.26	2.270	$t(36)=0.099; p = 0.922$	Equal
1.15	Training and education	2.22	2.237	$t(37)=0.190; p = 0.851$	Equal
1.16	Organizational learning	2.22	2.167	$t(38)=-0.571; p = 0.571$	Equal

Source: Own research.

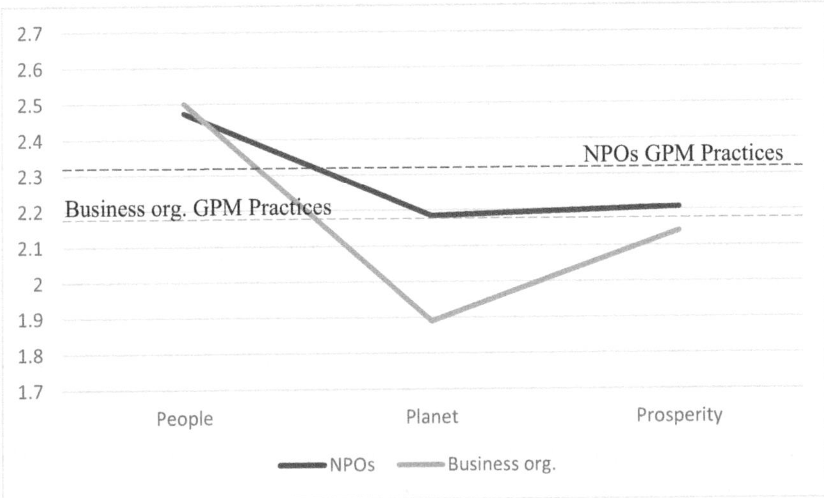

Figure 5.5 Comparison of the frequency with which the Green Project Management practices are exercised in NPOs and business organizations.

Source: Own research.

built this variable. It appears that there are statistically significant differences in the valuation of frequency of application of GPM practices for:

- *Duty or compulsion to work, Bribery limitation, Diversity and equal opportunities* and *Community support* – these variables were assessed significantly better by NPOs
- *Labor practices and decent work, Occupational health and safety in the project* – these variables, in turn, were assessed significantly worse by NPOs.

Interestingly, there is a certain convergence of the obtained results when it comes to business organizations and NPOs: in both cases, *Training and education* and *Organizational learning* were rated similarly poor.

Project management methodology and the frequency of application of GPM practices in NPOs

As a next step, in order to verify hypotheses H2a–c, correlation analysis between the applied project management methodology and *GPM Practices* (and its components) in NPOs was performed. Due to large disproportions in the sample size (17.5% – Agile methodologies; 82.5 % – traditional methodologies), a violation of the assumption regarding the normality of the *People* variable distribution and breaking the assumption of homogeneity of variance in the case of the

Table 5.6 Correlation analysis results – *PMM* and *GPM Practices*

Variable	*Non-linear correlation*							
	People		*Planet*		*Prosperity*		*GPM Practices*	
	N	*40*	*N*	*38*	*N*	*37*	*N*	*40*
Project Management Methodology (PMM)	η	0.038	η	0.130	η	0.099	η	0.053
	η^2	0.001	η^2	0.017	η^2	0.010	η^2	0.003
	$F(1.38) = 0.056$; $p = 0.814$ $U = 100.0$; $p = 0.601$		$F(1.36) = 0.614$; $p = 0.438$ $U = 138.5$; $p = 0.265$		$F(1.35) = 0.344$; $p = 0.561$ $U = 119.0$; $p = 0.608$		$F(1.38) = 0.107$; $p = 0.746$ $U = 135.0$; $p = 0.507$	

Source: Own research.

Prosperity and *GPM Practices* variables, non-parametric tests were used. The obtained results are presented in Table 5.6.

The obtained results show that there is no statistically significant relationship between the applied project management methodology and the frequency of application of *GPM Practices*; thus, hypotheses H2a–c must be rejected. This means that in the surveyed NPOs the frequency of application of GPM practices is similar regardless of whether they use traditional or agile methodologies.

Discussion of the findings

The aim of the conducted research was to determine the frequency with which the GPM practices are exercised in NPOs in Poland. An attempt was made to verify whether the frequency of application of the GPM practices significantly differs in NPOs and in business organizations, and whether application of specific project management methodologies fosters more frequent applications of GPM practices in the NPOs.

On the basis of the 3-point scale adopted in the research the frequency the GPM practices of GPM was rated at 2.31.

The score obtained in this study (2.31) is slightly higher than in business organizations (2.18) (Trocki et al., 2020), although it is worth noting, that the trend in the overall level of scores for individual areas (People, Planet, Prosperity) in NPOs is the same as in business organizations.

There is, however, a wide disparity in ratings across the NPOs surveyed. The best rated area was People and the lowest was Planet, while Prosperity did not fare much better than Planet. Respondents indicated that policies and procedures to protect the privacy of project participants are followed during projects, and legal solutions are in place to eliminate unethical behavior. Equal treatment of project participants regardless of their gender, age, political beliefs, religion, nationality, education etc. was also ensured. Project performance was assessed solely on the basis of skills and performance, and instances of unequal treatment of project participants were met with a fundamentally adequate response from management. It is likely that such good performance in these areas is enforced by the applicable legislation (public procurement law, anti-corruption law, EU equality directives, labor code, personal data protection law etc.). It is worth noting, however, that in areas that are not supported by such legal provisions, the frequency of application of GPM practices is lower.

The research shows that the examined NPOs had great problems with shaping systemic solutions supporting the collection and use of project experience, as they do not always collect, analyze and use the previous experience or the experience of other NPOs in the field of managing similar projects (e.g. as part of the NPO support network). This could also expand the scope of support for project participants (project managers, project team members, organization management, support units) for undertaking training and development activities, correlated with identified skill gaps and development needs. This is all the more important as research has shown that *Organizational learning* ($ß = 0.766$; $p < 0.001$) appeared to be the statistically important predictor of *Relations between employees and management*, and it accounted for a total of almost 57.5% of the variance in this variable. This model turned out to be a good fit to the data ($F(1.36) = 50.967$; $p < 0.001$).

Furthermore, it can be observed that of the three areas in which the frequency of application of GPM practices was assessed, the Planet area was rated lowest. One may be puzzled by the high percentage of responses indicating that the surveyed NPOs do not take into account such GPM-relevant issues as carbon footprint measurement (high number of "not applicable" responses) when implementing projects. It is likely that they do not identify for example, the problem of excessive GHG emissions during business trips by car or plane. This is in line with the results of surveys in the business sector (Trocki et al., 2020), where it was noted that in the Planet area, environmental aspects scored significantly lower than in the other areas. According to the authors of the study, this may be due to Poland's geopolitical location, cultural norms and attitudes to work, but may also be the result of low environmental awareness and sensitivity, and the ways in which human relations are formed. The surveyed NPOs also make little use of digital communication opportunities to reduce their carbon footprint and engage qualified staff wherever they are located. This is probably related to the low level of computerization of Polish NPOs (Klon/Jawor Association, 2021).

Referring to the applied project management methodology in the context of GPM, it can be noted that the obtained results indicate that there is no statistically significant relationship between the applied project management methodology and the frequency the GPM practices. This means that the surveyed organizations achieved a similar level of the frequency the GPM sustainable project management regardless of whether they used traditional or Agile methodologies. While this can be expected in the group of experienced organizations, it is surprising for organizations with little experience. This may be influenced by other factors, such as the fact that both very experienced and very inexperienced organizations choose Agile approaches to manage projects. However, as the number of organizations that indicated the use of Agile methodologies is relatively small in the sample, the obtained results should be treated with great caution and become the subject of further research, especially since there is a very limited number of works in this area in the global literature (Armenia et al., 2019; Chofreh et al., 2019; Kivilä et al., 2017).

Implications for future research

The identified problems, challenges and proposed solutions in the studied area indicate the necessity of expanding research. Despite the extensive body of GPM concepts, methods and good practices, this body of work is not sufficiently recognized among NPOs. It is, therefore, important to disseminate it. Motivation related to the popularization of GPM is needed here, which seems not to be problematic for NPOs. The context of the projects carried out, the participation of stakeholders and the reliance on shared values provide ample space for a GPM orientation.

The considerations presented here relate to a completely new topic, and it seems that research on these issues is only beginning to develop (Jałocha, 2014; Corboni et al., 2020). The results presented open the way for further research within GPM in NPOs. They may also shed light on the changes that await NPOs, including a stronger focus on environmental aspects in their operations. It is recommended that further research be conducted with a view to expanding knowledge in the area indicated and to clarify the above issues. Given the results obtained, it would be interesting to conduct research to identify success factors in the implementation of GPM, as well as to propose a model of NPO maturity in terms of GPM.

However, it should be noted that the research process implemented has its limitations. Respondents were asked to assess practices in sensitive areas of operation; hence, the likelihood of an inflated self-assessment was high. Other limitations relate to the survey methodology adopted. One of them is the size of the survey sample. This necessitates the assumption that the presented conclusions are tentative and should only refer to the research group. Another limitation is the adopted 3-point scale response. Its adoption was related to the adaptation of the prepared questionnaire form to the tools used in business entities. In further in-depth research, one should consider modifying this scale. Extending it would allow more interdependencies between GPM areas to be explored in NPOs. Another important limitation was the lack of answers to some questions. This was related to the large number of questions included in the questionnaire. Consequently, consideration could be given to aggregating some of the questions.

References

Alleman, G. (2005). "Agile Blog" email to Yahoo Groups, *Agile Project Management group.*

Armenia, S., Dangelico, R. M., Nonino, F., & Pompei, A. (2019). Sustainable project management: A conceptualization-oriented review and a framework proposal for future studies. *Sustainability*, *11*(9), 2664.

Casey, J. (2016). *The Nonprofit World: Civil Society and the Rise of the Nonprofit Sector*. Kumarian Press.

Chofreh, A. G., Goni, F. A., Malik, M. N., Khan, H. H., & Klemeš, J. J. (2019). The imperative and research directions of sustainable project management. *Journal of Cleaner Production,* 238, 117810. https://doi.org/10.1016/j.jclepro.2019.117810

Colás, A. (2013). *International Civil Society: Social Movements in World Politics*. John Wiley & Sons.

Corboni J., Duncan W., Gonzalez M., Milsom P., & Young M. (2020), Zrównoważone zarządzanie projektami. *Podręcznik GPM*. pm2pm.

Domański, J. (2012). Competitiveness of nongovernmental organizations in developing countries: Evidence from Poland. *Nonprofit Voluntary Sector Quarterly,* 41, 100–119. https://doi.org/10.1177/0899764010395947

Elkington, J., & Rowlands, I. H. (1999). Cannibals with forks: The triple bottom line of 21st century business. *Alternatives Journal, 25*(4), 42.

European Economic and Social Committee, (2022). www.eesc.europa.eu/pl/policies/policy-areas/sustainable-development/events (16.11.2022).

Gareis, R., Huemann, M., & Martinuzzi, A. (2011). What can project management learn from considering sustainability principles. *Project Perspectives, 33*(2), 60–65.

Golini, R., Kalchschmidt, M., & Landoni, P. (2015). Adoption of project management practices: The impact on international development projects of non-governmental organizations. *International Journal of Project Management, 33*(3), 650–663. https://doi.org/10.1016/j.ijproman.2014.09.006

GPM Global. (2014). *The GPM Global P5 Standard for Sustainability in Project Management*. People, planet and Profit, Project Processes and Products, The GPM 2014, www.greenprojectmanagement.org (24.02.2023).

Jałocha, B. (2014). *Zarządzanie portfelem projektów: koncepcje biznesowe a praktyka organizacji publicznych*. Kraków: Wydawnictwo Uniwersytetu Jagiellońskiego.

Jałocha, B., & Bogacz-Wojtanowska, E. (2017). Project portfolio management: Tool for strategy implementation in non-governmental organizations. In Lou, W. L. and Andrew, W. (Eds.), *Start-ups and SMEs: Concepts, Methodologies, Tools, and Applications* (pp. 547–563). Hershey : IGI Global. https://doi.org/10.4018/978-1-5225-25370.ch006

Juchniewicz M. (2019). Badanie społecznej odpowiedzialności działalności projektowej. In Trocki, M. (Ed.), *Społeczna odpowiedzialność działalności projektowej* (pp. 135–176). Warszawa: Oficyna Wydawnicza SGH.

Khang, D. B., & Moe, T. L. (2008). Success criteria and factors for international development projects: A life-cycle-based framework. *Project Management Journal, 39*(1), 72–84. https://doi.org/10.1002/pmj.20034

Kivilä, J., Martinsuo, M., & Vuorinen, L. (2017). Sustainable project management through project control in infrastructure projects. *International Journal of Project Management, 35*(6), 1167–1183. https://doi.org/10.1016/j.ijproman.2017.02.009

Klon/Jawor Association. (2021), Warsaw, July 2022, https://fakty.ngo.pl/raporty/the-capacity-of-ngos-in-poland-key-facts-2021 (24.02.2023).

Kloppenborg, T. J., & Opfer, W. A. (2002). The current state of project management research: Trends, interpretations, and predictions. *Project Management Journal, 33*(2), 5–18. https://doi.org/10.1177/875697280203300203

Licerán-Gutiérrez, A., Ortega-Rodríguez, C., Moreno-Albarracín, A. L., Labella, A., Rodríguez, R. M., & Martínez, L. (2022). A linguistic group best–worst method for measuring good governance in the third sector: A Spanish case study. *International Journal of Fuzzy Systems, 24*(5), 2133–2156. https://doi.org/10.1007/s40815-022-01274-3

Nagaria, J., Sadath, L., & Ahmed, S. (2019, March). Agile implementation-A milestone for academics using software engineering industry practices. In *2019 Advances in Science and Engineering Technology International Conferences (ASET)* (pp. 1–6). IEEE. https://doi.org/10.1109/ICASET.2019.8714575

Nieto-Rodriguez, A. (2012). *The Focused Organizations*. Gower.

Patrizia, G., & Massimo, R. (2014). Transparency in Italian nonprofit organizations. *Annals of Faculty of Economics, University of Oradea, Faculty of* Economics, *1*(1), 125–135.

Saidoun, A. (2020). Project Management Competences and the Sustainability of Non-profit Organisations. In Cuevas, R., Bodea, C.N., & Torres-Lima, P. (Eds), *Research on Project, Programme and Portfolio Management: Integrating Sustainability into Project Management* (pp. 301–312). Springer. https://doi.org/10.1007/978-3-030-60139-3_21

Salamon, L. M. (2010). The changing context of nonprofit leadership and management. In Renz, D. O. & Herman, R. D. (Eds.), *The Jossey-Bass Handbook of Nonprofit Leadership and Management* (pp. 77–100). John Wiley & Sons, Inc.

Salamon, L. M., & Sokolowski, S. W. (2016). Beyond nonprofits: Re-conceptualizing the third sector. *VOLUNTAS: International Journal of Voluntary and Nonprofit Organizations, 27*, 1515–1545.

Schoper, Y. G., Wald, A., Ingason, H. T., & Fridgeirsson, T. V. (2018). Projectification in Western economies: A comparative study of Germany, Norway and Iceland. *International Journal of Project Management, 36*(1), 71–82. https://doi.org/10.1016/j.ijproman.2017.07.008

Seiler, B., & Bortnowska, H. (2020). Mission statements and values of Polish non-profit organisations. *Organizacja i Zarządzanie: kwartalnik naukowy*, 117–146. https://doi.org/10.29119/1899-6116.2020.52.9

Shenhar, A. J., & Dvir, D. (2007). *Reinventing project management: The diamond approach to successful growth and innovation.* Harvard Business Review Press.

Silvius, A. G., & Schipper, R. (2010, November). A maturity model for integrating sustainability in projects and project management. In *24th World congress of the international project management association (IPMA) Istanbul, Turkey.*

Silvius, A. J., & Schipper, R. P. (2014). Sustainability in project management: A literature review and impact analysis. *Social Business, 4*(1), 63–96. https://doi.org/10.1362/204440814X13948909253866

Sońta-Drączkowska, E., & Mrożewski, M. (2020). Exploring the role of project management in product development of new technology-based firms. *Project Management Journal, 51*(3), 294–311. https://doi.org/10.1177/8756972819851939

Subedi, S., & Wagner, R. (2018). Portfolio management in non-governmental organizations. In Lock, D., & Wagner, R. (Eds.), *The Handbook of Project Portfolio Management* (pp. 143–152). London: Routledge. https://doi.org/10.4324/9781315206592

Transforming our World: the 2030 Agenda for Sustainability Development A/RES/70/1, United Nations 2015, https://sustainabledevelopment.un.org/post2015/transformingourworld/publication (30.01.2023).

Trocki, M. (2020), *Organizacja projektowa*. PWE.

Trocki, M., & Juchniewicz, M. (2017). Social responsibility of projects–the essence and results of survey. In Teczke, J. & Buła, P. (Eds.). *Management in the Time of Networks, Cross-cultural Activities and Flexible Organisations* (pp. 353–366). International Management Foundation, Cracow University of Economics.

Trocki, M., Juchniewicz, M., & Bukłaha, E. (2020). Socially responsible project management. *Journal of Management and Financial Sciences,* (41), 45–60. https://doi.org/10.33119/JMFS.2020.41.3

Waters, R. D., & Ott, H. K. (2014). Corporate social responsibility and the nonprofit sector: Assessing the thoughts and practices across three nonprofit subsectors. *Public Relations Journal*, *8*(3). www.prsa.org/Intelligence/PRJournal/Vol8/No3/

Wawak, S., & Woźniak, K. (2020). Evolution of project management studies in the XXI century. *International Journal of Managing Projects in Business*, *13*(4), 867–888. https://doi.org/10.1108/IJMPB-01-2020-0002

Whitelock, V. G. (2019). Multidimensional environmental social governance sustainability framework: Integration, using a purchasing, operations, and supply chain management context. *Sustainable Development*, *27*(5), 923–931. https://doi.org/10.1002/sd.1951

Zakrzewska, M., Piwowar-Sulej, K., Jarosz, S., Sagan, A., & Sołtysik, M. (2022). The linkage between Agile project management and sustainable development: A theoretical and empirical view. *Sustainable Development*, *30*(5), 855–869. https://doi.org/10.1002/sd.2285

6 The evolution of project managers' competencies and leadership styles

The agility and sustainability contexts

Katarzyna Grzesik and Katarzyna Piwowar-Sulej

Standards of practice in the area of project managers' competencies and leadership styles

The extant literature shows that project managers' competencies are of utmost importance for a project's success (Alvarenga *et al.*, 2019; Eger & Egerová, 2016; Grzesik & Piwowar-Sulej, 2018). They can be defined as a combination of knowledge, attitudes, skills and other personal characteristics that affect the effectiveness and efficiency of project management. They can be measured against accepted standards and be developed through training and workshops (PMI, 2017a). According to International Project Management Association (IPMA) a project manager's competence is the application of knowledge, skills and abilities to achieve a project outcome (IPMA, 2015). What is also important is that for years it has been argued that there is a greater need for leadership than the need for management in the context of projects (e.g., Anantatmula, 2010; Bhatti *et al.*, 2021; Day, 1998; Turner & Müller, 2005). Leadership is the "accomplishment of a goal through the direction of human assistants" (Prentice, 2004). Relations with people are more important than technical skills here. Therefore, the development of so-called "soft" competencies of project managers has gained popularity among practitioners and researchers. Furthermore, one can find a notion of leadership competencies that are a combination of knowledge, skills and personality characteristics that leads to superior results (Crawford, 2005). Finally, literature distinguishes many leadership styles defined as stable patterns of leaders' behaviors. These leadership styles have also been a subject of analyses conducted by researchers (e.g., Ali *et al.*, 2021).

The issue of project managers' competencies is presented both in the standards of practice and by the research results. Guidelines, frameworks or standards developed by project management institutions can be used to identify competencies and identify guidelines for developing the necessary project management competencies. Some of the most popular models developed by project management institutions include:

- the *Individual Competence Baseline for Project Programme and Portfolio Management* (ICB) created by the International Project Management Association (IPMA),

DOI: 10.4324/9781003356059-7

- the *Project Management Competency Development* (PMCD) created by the Project Management Institute (PMI),
- the *PMI Talent Triangle* introduced by PMBOK Guide (*A Guide to the Project Management Body of Knowledge*) by the Project Management Institute (PMI),
- the *APM Competence Framework* (ACF) developed by the Association for Project Management (APM).

The guidelines created by the above-presented institutions and project management associations bring a comprehensive view of the main competencies that a project manager should strive for in order to effectively manage a project. The available practice standards and frameworks present various competencies of project managers and categorize them.

Individual Competence Baseline for Project Programme and Portfolio Management Version 4.0 (ICB.4) introduces 28 competencies of project managers in three groups (IPMA, 2015):

- people—10 competencies: self-reflection and self-management; personal integrity and reliability; personal communication; relationships and engagement; leadership; teamwork; conflict and crisis; resourcefulness; negotiation; result orientation,
- practice—13 competencies: project design; requirements and objectives; scope; time; organization and information; quality; finance; resource; procurement; plan and control; risk and opportunity; stakeholders, change and transformation,
- perspective—5 competencies: strategy; governance, structure and processes; compliance, standard and regulation; power and interest; culture and values.

What is important is that leadership was placed among competencies related to people management. However, values or strategy—that play important role in leadership (Carter & Greer, 2013)—have been placed in an another group of competencies, i.e., "perspective".

The first integrated standards for project management competencies did not appear until the mid-1990s. In 1997, IPMA launched the first version of its *Individual Competence Baseline for Project Programme and Portfolio Management* (ICB.1). An improved second version (ICB.2) followed in 1999 and a third one (ICB.3) in 2006, and fourth version (ICB.4) was announced for release in 2015. In the development of the ICB, competencies addressing the behavioral and change aspects of projects and the context of projects got increasing attention.

In *Project Management Competency Development* (PMCD) 16 mentioned competencies of project managers are divided into two groups (PMI, 2017a):

- performance—10 competencies: project integration management; project scope management; project time management; project cost management; project quality management; project human resource management; project communication management; project risk management; project procurement management; project stakeholder management,

- personal—6 competencies: communicating; leading; managing; cognitive ability; effectiveness; professionalism.

Leading was placed next to communication, whereas academic literature shows that one of the basic leadership skills is communication that allows to build trust and encourage followers (Barrett, 2006).

In turn, *PMI Talent Triangle* considers three types of project managers' skills (PMI, 2017b):

- technical project management,
- leadership,
- strategic and business management.

Finally, *APM Competence Framework* (ACF) considers 11 competencies in two groups (APM, 2012):

- interpersonal—7 competencies: communication; conflict management; delegation; influencing; leadership; negotiation; teamwork,
- professional—4 competencies: communities of practice; competence; ethics framework; leading and development.

It is puzzling why influencing is next to leadership, whereas in fact leadership is about influencing people.

As above presented, proposed by project management institutions and associations the content of the standards of practices in the area of project managers' competencies are somewhat different. If there are discrepancies between the standards of practices, it seems probable that there may be some discrepancies between the content of the standards of practice and research results on project managers' competencies. Occurrence of discrepancies between standards of practices became the basis for a study conducted by Moradi *et al.* (2020). Their analyses show that there are four discrepancies between research results on project managers' competencies and standards of practice (Moradi *et al.*, 2020):

- some competencies are missing in the standards of practice,
- there is a mismatch between research results and standards of practice concerning priority of some project managers' competencies,
- there is uneven degree of consensus over the importance of some project managers' competencies between research results and the standards of practice,
- research results are more context-oriented than the standards of practice over project managers' competencies.

The PMBOK lists six leadership styles as most common used in projects among the numerous leadership styles presented in the literature on general management (PMI, 2017b). They are: transformational, transactional, laissez-faire, charismatic, servant and interactional. Transactional leadership style is based on the exchange relationship occurring between the leader and group members. A transactional leader encourages subordinates to complete assigned tasks and rewards them for the desired behavior. Such a leader is focused on goals, feedback and accomplishment to determine rewards (Bass, 1990). Transactional leadership is often contrasted with transformational leadership. However, transactional and transformational leadership should not be viewed as opposing approaches, as transformational leadership is built on the foundation of transactional leadership. Transformational leadership style involves developing an inspiring vision and uniting employees around it. In this style, the team is willing to transform and evolve to achieve the overall goal (Bass & Riggio, 2006). Transformational leadership is complemented by charismatic leadership. Charismatic leadership assumes that the individual characteristic of a leader is charisma. Charismatic leaders influence the actions of their followers, through their personality traits they inspire others to go beyond self-interest for the good of the organization. A combination of transactional, transformational and charismatic is seen by the PMBOK as an interactional style. Another example of a leadership style is the laissez-faire style, which involves empowering employees, being hands-off, and trusting them to accomplish the task at hand without constant questions while staying available to provide feedback when necessary. This leadership style allowing the team to make their own decisions and establish their own goals (Avolio *et al.*, 1999). While traditional leadership generally involves the accumulation and exercise of power by a leader, servant leadership is different (Greenleaf, 2002). The servant-leader shares power, puts the needs of others first and focuses on other people's growth, learning, development, autonomy as highly as possible. Servant leadership is about empowering team and helping create a positive work environment.

Project managers' competencies and leadership as subjects of research

Over the last few decades, a large number of research studies have been carried out on project managers' (called often project leaders) competencies, since—as presented earlier—they are the critical factors of project performance. Some of these studies have addressed project managers' competencies in general and some other studies have focused on a specific context or project type to find competencies of relevance for project managers. What is also interesting is that there is a limited number of literature reviews to synthesize research studies on project managers' competencies.

In the research conducted by Moradi *et al.* (2020), key project managers' competencies were identified and ranked based on competencies present in the previous studies and standards of practice. The list of project managers' competencies mentioned by previous studies and standards of practice from 1959 to 2018 includes 98 competencies. It was also found that 68 out of those 98 competencies can be classified as weighty competencies with respect of their appearance and likely importance for the success of project. According to the total frequency of appearance in both previous studies and standards of practice, the following main competencies were identified (frequency of appearance): communication (25), leadership (19), teamwork and cooperation (14), flexibility (12), problem-solving (12), goal orientation (12), developing others (11), impact and influence (11), stakeholder management (11), cost management (11), resource management (11), analytical thinking (10), quality management (9), risk management (9), conflict management (9), ethics (9), decision making (8), time management (8), planning (8), experience (7), technical competencies (7), procurement management (7), scope management (7), team management (6), creativity (6), conceptual thinking (6), project management (6), change management (6), strategic direction (6), negotiation (6) and cultural skills (6).

The 11 competencies shown in Figure 6.1 have been identified as project managers' key competencies (with more than 10 appearances in the previous studies and standards of practice) that contribute to project success more than other identified competencies in the study (Moradi *et al.*, 2020). These competencies can be considered as project managers' core competencies in general (for all project types and targets). The key competencies of project managers have continuously been important and demanding since 2001 (see Figure 6.1).

Figure 6.1 shows the appearance trend of project managers' key competencies during recent decades. The diagram shown indicates the increasing importance of social competencies such as communication, leadership, and teamwork and cooperation. The situation presented is related to the practice of project management, which in recent years has been undergoing an evolution from the traditional approach based on predictability and classic planning to an agile approach that emphasizes adaptability, creativity and rapid customer-oriented action. These

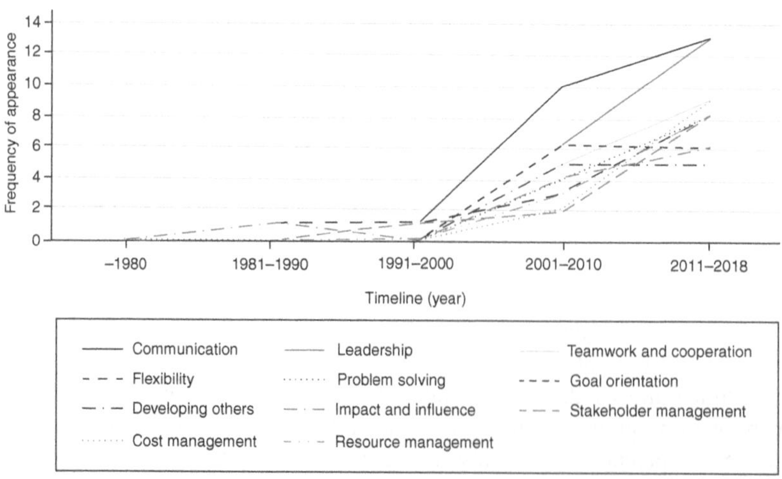

Figure 6.1 Chronological presentation of project managers' key competencies' frequency of appearance.

Source: Moradi *et al.* (2020, p. 555).

changes have also resulted in a shift in the role of the project manager and, consequently, the competencies expected of him or her.

As far as literature reviews on project managers' competencies and leadership are concerned, Ahmed *et al.* (2021) classified the analyzed competencies in the following order (starting with the highest first and decreasing in order thereafter): communication (14), developing/growth (13), achieving (12), critical analysis (12), empowering (12), managing resources (12), strategic perspective (12), conscientiousness (11), engaging (11), influence (11), motivation (11), sensitivity (11), vision and imagination (11), emotional resilience (10), intuitiveness (10), self-awareness (10), attentiveness (5), managerial expertise (5), knowledge sharing (5), effectiveness (3), administrative expertise (3), teamwork (3), PM expertise (3), monitor (3), producer (3), cognitive ability (2), decision-making (2), helping relationship (2), managing conflict (2), facilitator (2), innovator (2), integrator (2), task proficient (2), extraversion (1), openness (1), mentor (1), broker (1), coordinator (1), director (1), interpersonal skills (1), experience (1), communicating expectations (1), defining roles and responsibilities (1), establishing trust (1) and personal characteristics (1). Then, the authors grouped these competencies into three main clusters: relationship-oriented, innovation-oriented and task-oriented (see Figure 6.2).

The systematic literature review of project manager's leadership competencies revealed that (Ahmed *et al.*, 2021):

- there is an ambiguity with respect to competencies and leadership styles when both terms are interchangeably used to capture and define project manager's role,
- leadership competencies have not been categorized or prioritized and researchers have used multiple but limited measurement tools and methods to examine the influence of project manager's competencies and leadership styles.

One can state that the project manager's role is evolving and should be strengthened with a broad range of knowledge and skills that are complementary to the traditional functions of project administration in order to acquire other competencies that modern project management requires. Context changes, such as an increase in project complexity, requirement of sustainability, the existence of multicultural issues and the growth of work by virtual teams have led to a new era in which project managers' personal competencies are increasingly crucial to the achievement of project success. The demand for soft skills is even more pronounced in project management than in other business environments (Ballesteros-Sánchez *et al.*, 2019).

Agility in project managers' competencies and leadership

Agility can be defined as "the ability of an organization to sense or create environmental change and respond efficiently and effectively to that change" (Gartner, 2006, p. 1). Agile Project Management (APM) is becoming a desirable response to fast-changing and challenging business environment and it can be found most

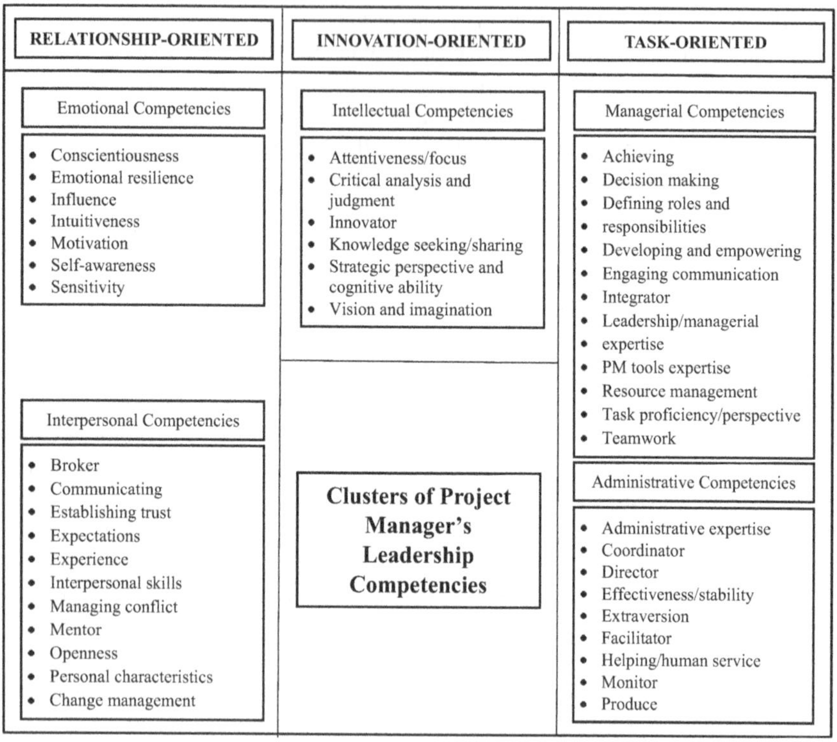

Figure 6.2 Clusters of project manager's leadership competencies.

Source: Ahmed *et al.* (2021, p. 20).

frequently in literature related to software development. However, other types of projects share many of the challenges that APM solved in software development therefore the number of project managers and business experts who recommend the implementation of APM to manage projects and teams outside the software industry is growing (Ciric *et al.*, 2019).

The approach to project management represented by traditional management methodologies places a strong emphasis primarily on planning and monitoring the execution of the established plan. The leadership style used for traditional project management is some version of command and control (Fischer & Charef, 2021). The main idea behind agility and the values of APM can be found in The Agile Manifesto (Agilemanifesto.org, 2020). Agile's founders emphasize the value of people, running product instead of extensive documentation, dynamic planning, working with clients on contract negotiations, real measurement of work progress and responding to changes resulting from a plan. Good communication, which is the foundation of the agile approach, requires a strong emphasis on personal elements and an understanding of organizational roles (Coplien & Harrison, 2005).

Referring to the tasks of project managers, it should be noted that in traditional project management, managers are primarily focused on the budget, schedule and scope of the project. The project manager in an agile approach, on the other hand, is focused on delivering results, and traditional project constraints are treated as secondary in this case. Similar differences can be seen in the approach to the project team. In traditional projects, it is easier to support the work of the team with well-defined project goals and needs and good documentation of the project. In an agile approach, teams must have a very high degree of flexibility to deal with changes immediately and deliver results quickly to the principal. In addition, it is essential that teams are able to flexibly reorganize and change their organizational roles. Team members should be characterized by a special level of commitment and be ready to make a special effort.

Increasingly, the role performed, as well as knowledge, skills and other predispositions, are linked to social competence. The manager is increasingly expected to play the role of a visionary and leader who can effectively coordinate the work of the entire team, consisting of people with high and varied competencies. The essence of team leadership in APM is based on the fact that project managers act more as mediators and coaches and less as authorities who make all decisions and try to control change in the first place (Piwowar-Sulej, 2021).

In response to the requirements of agility, Appelo (2011) created a concept of project leadership called Management 3.0. This concept comprises six pillars: (1) energizing people, (2) empowering teams, (3) aligning constraints (through, e.g., setting a well-defined goal), (4) developing competence, (5) growing structure (creating a friendly, scalable work environment) and (6) improving everything. Each pillar is equally as important as the others. Moreover, many practical tools have been created to help managers act in accordance with these pillars.

According to the principles of Management 3.0, agile project managers should provide adequate support for the team in which they work. They do not have to be the best and the smartest in the technical fields in which they work, but they must be able to support people working in their team and improve the team (McPherson, 2016). They should cope with challenges without knowing the detail, get quickly to grips with complex issues and ask the right questions (McPherson, 2016).

APM also stresses the use of servant leadership (Fischer & Charef, 2021). Finally, literature also distinguishes smart leadership which is about being agile and flexible. It covers creating an exciting and compelling vision and inspiring people to deliver on it. Smart leaders energize people and ignite to unleash and exploit their potential. They develop their teams based on previous experience and novel knowledge. They are resilient in times of volatility and uncertainty, forward thinking and are anticipatory (Iannotta *et al.*, 2020). One can find here some similarities with transformational leadership style and the concept of Management 3.0. Rao (2013) emphasized that smart leadership is mainly based on appropriate balancing between soft power (i.e., attracting people), and hard power (i.e., using punishments and rewards). However, to date a required competency framework for APM has not been created. Existing agile-related professional body publications are primarily guidelines. For example, the Agile Practice

Guide of the PMI (2017c) provides general guidelines and an understanding of Agile approaches and a framework, tools and techniques that project teams can use and explains how to create and deliver a project in an agile environment to deliver valuable results to their customers. Other professional bodies, such as the IPMA (2018), published an Agile reference guide in 2018, which goes further to clarify the need of Agile leaders and explains how different Agile elements (perspective, people and practice) translate into observable competencies in an Agile environment (Ahsan & Ho, 2022).

Sustainability in project managers' competencies and leadership

Since the implementation of sustainability—"a paradigm for thinking about the future in which environmental, societal, and economic considerations are balanced in the pursuit of an improved quality of life" (Jeronen, 2013)—is one of the most important challenges of our time, it has also been linked to project management. Projects are "instruments of change" in organizations that play an important role in implementing sustainable business processes and practices (Silvius & Schipper, 2014). Integrating sustainability into project management not only affects project management processes and practices, but also the competencies of the project manager. The sustainability perspective evolved into the concept of Sustainable Project Management that is considered one of the most important global project management trends today. Most recently, research exploring the role of the project manager has identified the central and influential position project managers hold regarding decisions over sustainability matters (Marnewick *et al.*, 2019; Poon & Silvius, 2019; Silvius & Schipper, 2020). The project manager's central position in the project offers the opportunity to steer the project toward multiple objectives (Sabini & Alderman, 2021). Therefore, it is necessary to understand what competencies the integration of sustainability into projects and project management would require of a project manager (Silvius *et al.*, 2012).

As above presented, the concept of competencies is not new to the project management profession, as there are well-developed standards for project management competencies. However, as earlier studies concluded, the standards for project management fail to address the enabling role of projects in sustainability. The conclusion that project management standards fail to address sustainability was clearly found by Eid in the book *Sustainable Development & Project Management* (Eid, 2009). The author of this book studied the integration of sustainable development in construction project management. Based on research findings he formulated the following conclusions:

- project management processes and knowledge fall short of committing to a sustainable approach,
- mapping sustainable development onto project management processes and knowledge areas identifies several opportunities for introducing sustainability guidelines into all project management processes.

In turn, Silvius and Schipper (2014) in their literature review covered competencies required to incorporate sustainability aspects, in project management competency standards. As the competency standards they adopted ICB.3 framework of technical, behavioral and contextual competencies. And as the competencies required for considering sustainability aspects they adopted the framework of key competencies of sustainability by Wick *et al.* (2011) as a suitable framework for consideration of sustainability competencies in project management competencies. This framework identifies five groups of competencies: systems thinking competencies, anticipatory competencies, normative competencies, strategic competencies and interpersonal competencies (Wiek, *et al.*, 2011):

- systems thinking competencies—refer to the ability to understand the intermediate and root causes of complex (sustainability) problems. This competence means the ability to collectively analyze complex problems across different domains (society, environment, economy, etc.) and across different scales (local to global). Such ability includes comprehending, empirically verifying and articulating their structure, key components and dynamics. The capacity to analyze is based on acquired systemic knowledge including concepts such as structure, function, cause-effect relations, but also perceptions, motives, decisions and regulations as well as methods and methodologies such as qualitative and quantitative modeling;
- anticipatory competencies—refer to the capacity to think systematically about the future and future generations. This competence is the ability to collectively analyze, evaluate and craft rich "pictures" of the future related to sustainability issues and sustainability problem-solving frameworks. The ability to analyze pictures of the future includes being able to comprehend and articulate their structure, key components and dynamics. The capacities to analyze, evaluate and craft are based on acquired future-oriented knowledge including concepts such as time and uncertainty as well as methods and methodologies such as simulation and scenario analysis;
- normative competencies—refer to the understanding of concepts of justice, equity, social-ecological integrity and ethics; and to the understanding how these concepts may vary across and within cultures. This competence is the ability to collectively map, specify, apply, reconcile and negotiate sustainability values, principles, goals and targets. Such capacity is based on acquired normative knowledge including concepts of justice, equity, social-ecological integrity and ethics as well as methods and methodologies such as multi-criteria assessment and structured visioning;
- strategic competencies—refer to the ability to collaboratively design and implement interventions and governance strategies with the sophistication necessary to address sustainability challenges. This capacity requires an intimate understanding of strategic concepts such as intentionality, systemic inertia, path dependencies, barriers, carriers, alliances etc.; knowledge about viability, feasibility, effectiveness, efficiency of systemic interventions as well as a potential of unintended consequences as well as methods and methodologies of designing,

testing, implementing, evaluating and adapting policies, programs and action plans, involving different societal actors, facilitating varying perspectives and acknowledging inconclusive evidence;
- interpersonal competencies—refer to the capacity to motivate and facilitate sustainability research and problem-solving. This capacity includes advanced skills in communicating, deliberating and negotiating, collaborating, leadership, pluralistic and trans-cultural thinking and empathy. All of these skills are particularly important for successful stakeholder collaboration and a necessity for the majority of methods assigned to previous competencies. The capacity to understand, embrace and facilitate diversity across cultures, social groups, communities and individuals is recognized as a key component of this competence.

Their research results showed how the key sustainability competencies are covered by the ICB.3: the systems thinking competencies are partly covered by the ICB.3 project management contextual competencies; the anticipatory competencies are not covered by the ICB.3 project management competencies; the normative competencies are only limitedly covered in the ICB.3 behavioral competencies; the strategic competencies are well covered in the ICB.3 technical competencies; and the interpersonal competencies are well covered in the ICB.3 behavioral competencies (Silvius & Schipper, 2014).

In response to the need to deal with sustainability issues sustainable leadership concept has emerged. This is because the new challenge for today's organizational leaders is to effectively lead their organizations through volatile economic times and address the topic of sustainability. As a result, the need to explore and define the concept of sustainable leadership is gaining importance (McCann & Holt, 2010). Sustainable leadership has several attributes that overlap with other theories of leadership, but also has its own distinctive elements. A synthesis of various concepts that present the idea of the essence of sustainable leadership reveals common features, which include: (1) emphasis on leadership rather than a specific leader, (2) long-term vision, (3) broader goals that link organizations to society, (4) ethical behavior, (5) social responsibility of leaders and organizations, (6) capacity for innovation, (7) systemic change, (8) stakeholder engagement, and (9) stakeholder capacity building of stakeholder (Hallinger & Suriyankietkaew, 2018).

Some of the characteristics of sustainable leadership mentioned in the literature overlap with elements of other leadership styles, such as transformational leadership, servant leadership or ethical leadership that weakens the distinctiveness of the sustainable leadership concept (Lee, 2017). However, an analysis of the distinguishing features of this leadership concept points to five attributes that more or less clearly distinguish the concept of sustainable leadership from other leadership concepts (Lee, 2017):

- diversity—in the concept of sustainable leadership, "everyone matters," meaning that sustainable leadership recognizes the value of having a diverse workforce to learn from other diverse practices. Additionally, it is accepted that standardization of work practices is the enemy of sustainability. For a company to grow, it must be able to innovate and come up with creative ways to achieve results. Innovation can be fostered when an enterprise maintains a diverse workforce. Employees with different aptitudes, experiences or backgrounds can bring different perspectives and knowledge necessary to solve organizational problems;

- organizational justice—leaders recognize that each individual matters to long-term prosperity, and that prosperity achieved at the expense of the well-being of individual groups cannot sustain itself. The benefits of one person can jeopardize the benefits of others in the company or in society, so sustainable leaders should be careful when making decisions that affect the interests of many people in the company, making every effort to ensure justice within the organization. All four dimensions of organizational justice are closely linked to employee well-being, which is critical to an organization's long-term performance. It should also be emphasized that ethical practices and maintaining high moral standards are important for long-term productivity, long-term commitment and employee loyalty. Sustainable leaders are proactive in addressing social justice issues;
- employee development—sustainable leaders view the people in a company as an asset to be nurtured and maintained, rather than a resource to be replaced. From the perspective of sustainable leadership, employee development in a company is a critical factor in achieving sustainable competitive advantage. Sustainable leadership takes into account the development of each employee on a continuous basis, so a company should continually develop and train its employees to be able to successfully perform new and challenging tasks;
- progress orientation—sustainable leaders care not only about the quality of current performance, but also about the possibility of progress. Therefore, they view current performance evaluations as an indication of what should be done in the future and provide constructive suggestions to learn from the past. This is the result of a constant effort to ensure that employees learn continuously. Organizational learning is essential to meet the demands of corporate sustainability;
- work-life balance—sustainable leaders realize that employees are a capital that is prone to depletion when abused or overused. Therefore, they pay special attention to the issue of work-life balance. The result is the implementation of work-life balancing. The rationale behind these programs is to increase company productivity by allowing employees to focus on their work, attracting talented candidates and reducing the turnover rate.

While leadership research in the past has been focused on behaviors, interactions, attributes, competencies and styles, contemporary leadership researchers are developing value-oriented leadership theories, among others (Chen & Li, 2013). Examples of such leadership theories include ethical leadership, responsible leadership, servant leadership and sustainable leadership that are being studied in relation to sustainability and project management (e.g., Muff *et al.*, 2020; Bilal *et al.*, 2021; Chamtitigul & Li, 2021; Mubarak *et al.*, 2022; Nauman *et al.*, 2022).

Another aspect concerning the perception of the essence of leadership is the paradigm shift from leadership, which is primarily the achievement of one leader, to leadership, which is the achievement of the collective. According to this paradigm, leadership is not understood as a property of the individual, but as a property of the system. This means that there is a shift away from leadership understood as a role to collective influence, relationships and mutual interdependence, which has resulted in the following leadership concepts: distributed leadership (Gronn, 2002; Woods, 2004; Harris, 2011), shared leadership (Pearce *et al.*, 2008; Zhu *et al.*, 2018), empowering leadership (Srivastava *et al.*, 2006; Vecchio *et al.*, 2010). Sustainable leadership also aligns with the idea of collective forms of leadership as a manifestation of more sustainable organizational practices (Avery & Bergsteiner, 2011). Sustainable leaders consider a wider stakeholder group and ensure the delivery of results that meet the triple bottom line of environmental, financial and social performance (Avery & Bergsteiner, 2011). When working with stakeholders they follow behaviors of responsible, transformational, empowering, servant and ethical leaders (Iqbal & Piwowar-Sulej, 2022). No sustainable project can exist without calling on the ethical aspect of the project manager and his team. In fact, it is already accepted as a fundamental skill in project administrator training and accreditation according to the most extensive standards (Marcelino-Sádaba *et al.*, 2015).

Implications for future research

The above presented analyses allow for the formulation of many interesting research avenues. First, the cited authors proposed some directions for future research. For example, Ahmed *et al.* (2021) revealed that a number of terms have been used widely in the literature in the context of project manager's potential and abilities. They include competencies, leadership styles, profiles, dimensions, roles and factors. These terms are having different concepts and meanings but are being used simultaneously in the literature regarding project manager's job. Different interpretations hinder the implementation of effective strategies for ensuring project outcomes are fully realized. Future researchers should, therefore, put emphasis on the boundaries between the earlier listed terms and use them in a consistent manner.

Second, since modern, agile project managers play a role of leader, coach or mentor, and are responsible for the development of project team members, there is a need to make them familiar with methods and principles applied in adult education, which falls within the domain of andragogy. A question arises on how to successfully develop project managers' competencies not only in this area (Piwowar-Sulej, 2021).

Third, Muller and Turner (2007) concluded that the project manager's leadership style influences project success, and different leadership styles may be appropriate for different types of projects. Špundak (2014) states that there are factors other than the characteristics of projects that determine the choice of project management methodology. The same can be referred to project leadership style because there is an association between project management methodology and project leadership style (Piwowar-Sulej, 2021). One should consider in future research, e.g., the relationship between the corporate culture of organization in which projects are managed and practiced in different leadership styles.

Fourth, factors inducing project managers to include sustainable objectives arise from many different influences. Silvius and Schipper (2020) argue that understanding the human behavior of the project manager can benefit the sustainable project management literature by providing an individual perspective. The main contribution of this recent stream of literature is that project managers, when considering or embedding sustainability in their projects are influenced by different factors: intrinsic motivation, compliance (task-driven) and pragmatism (Silvius & Schipper, 2020). Therefore, future research is needed on the linkage between these factors and the level of project manager's competencies as well as the practiced leadership styles.

Fifth, in the context of agile and sustainable project management, it is worth examining the emerging leadership styles, which are called Management 3.0 and sustainable leadership respectively. Both of them are rather in theoretical stage of development. There is also a lack of measurement instruments to use when investigating these project leadership styles in business.

Finally, taking into account different leadership styles, one can state that transformational leadership corresponds with different project management approaches. Although servant or shared leadership seems to be relevant in terms of fulfilling the postulates of agile approach, there are studies which link this leadership to APM (Malik *et al.*, 2023). Moreover, general management literature shows that various leadership styles are effective in stimulating organizational sustainable performance (Piwowar-Sulej & Iqbal, 2022). Therefore, future studies should focus on making comparisons between different leadership styles in terms of their effectiveness related to different project management approaches.

References

Agilemanifesto.org. (2020). *Agile Manifesto*. https://agilemanifesto.org/

Ahmed, R., Philbin, S. P., & Cheema, F. E. A. (2021). Systematic literature review of project manager's leadership competencies. *Engineering, Construction and Architectural Management*, *28*(1), 1–30. https://doi.org/10.1108/ECAM-05-2019-0276

Ahsan, K., & Ho, M. (2022). Analysis of agile project manager competencies from recruitment signals. *IEEE Transactions on Engineering Management*, *71*, 1–14. https://doi.org/10.1109/TEM.2022.3222037

Ali, H., Chuanmin, S., Ahmed, M., Mahmood, A., Khayyam, M., & Tikhomirova, A. (2021). Transformational leadership and project success: Serial mediation of team-building and teamwork. *Frontiers in Psychology*, *12*. https://doi.org/10.3389/fpsyg.2021.689311

Alvarenga, J. C., Branco, R. R., Guedes, A. L. A., Soares, C. A. P., & Silva, W. da S. e. (2019). The project manager core competencies to project success. *International Journal of Managing Projects in Business*, *13*(2), 277–292. https://doi.org/10.1108/IJMPB-12-2018-0274

Anantatmula, V. S. (2010). Project manager leadership role in improving project performance. *Engineering Management Journal*, *22*(1), 13–22. https://doi.org/10.1080/10429247.2010.11431849

Appelo, J. (2011). *Leading Agile Developers, Developing Agile Leaders*. Addison-Wesley Professional, Boston.

Association for Project Management (APM). (2012). APM Body of Knowledge, Buckinghamshire, UK.

Avery, G. C., & Bergsteiner, H. (2011). Sustainable leadership practices for enhancing business resilience and performance. *Strategy & Leadership*, *39*(3), 5–15. https://doi.org/10.1108/10878571111128766

Avolio, B. J., Bass, B. M., & Jung, D. I. (1999). Re-examining the components of transformational and transactional leadership using the Multifactor Leadership. *Journal of occupational and organizational psychology*, *72*(4), 441–462. https://doi.org/10.1348/096317999166789

Ballesteros-Sánchez, L., Ortiz-Marcos, I., & Rodríguez-Rivero, R. (2019). The impact of executive coaching on project managers' personal competencies. *Project Management Journal*, *50*(3), 306–321. https://doi.org/10.1177/8756972819832191

Barrett, D. J. (2006). Strong communication skills a must for today's leaders. *Handbook of Business Strategy*, *7*(1), 385–390. https://doi.org/10.1108/10775730610619124

Bass, B. M. (1990). From transactional to transformational leadership: Learning to share the vision. *Organizational dynamics*, *18*(3), 19–31. https://doi.org/10.1016/0090-2616(90)90061-S

Bass, B. M., & Riggio, R. E. (2006). *Transformational Leadership*. Psychology Press, New York.

Bhatti, S. H., Kiyani, S. K., Dust, S. B., & Zakariya, R. (2021). The impact of ethical leadership on project success: the mediating role of trust and knowledge sharing. *International Journal of Managing Projects in Business*, *14*(4), 982–998. https://doi.org/10.1108/IJMPB-05-2020-0159

Bilal, A., Siddiquei, A., Asadullah, M. A., Awan, H. M., & Asmi, F. (2021). Servant leadership: A new perspective to explore project leadership and team effectiveness. *International Journal of Organizational Analysis*, *29*(3), 699–715. https://doi.org/10.1108/IJOA-12-2019-1975

Carter, S. M., & Greer, C. R. (2013). Strategic leadership. *Journal of Leadership & Organizational Studies*, *20*(4), 375–393. https://doi.org/10.1177/1548051812471724

Chamtitigul, N., & Li, W. (2021). The influence of ethical leadership and team learning on team performance in software development projects. *Team Performance Management: An International Journal*. https://doi.org/10.1108/TPM-02-2020-0014

Chen, C. Y., & Li, C. I. (2013). Assessing the spiritual leadership effectiveness: The contribution of follower's self– concept and preliminary tests for moderation of culture and managerial position. *The Leadership Quarterly*, *24*(1), 240–255. https://doi.org/10.1016/j.leaqua.2012.11.004

Ciric, D., Lalic, B., Gracanin, D., Tasic, N., Delic, M., & Medic, N. (2019). Agile vs. Traditional approach in project management: Strategies, challenges and reasons to introduce agile. *Procedia Manufacturing, 39*, 1407–1414. https://doi.org/10.1016/j.promfg.2020.01.314

Coplien, J., & Harrison, N. (2005). *Organizational Patterns of Agile Software Development*. Pearson Prentice Hall, New York.

Crawford, L. (2005). Senior management perceptions of project management competence. *International Journal of Project Management*, *23*(1), 7–16. https://doi.org/10.1016/j.ijproman.2004.06.005

Day, R. M. (1998). Leadership of fast track projects. *IEEE Aerospace Conference Proceedings (Cat. No.98TH8339)*, Snowmass, CO, USA, pp. 433–442, vol. 5, doi: 10.1109/AERO.1998.685853.

Eger, L., & Egerová, D. (2016). Project risk management in educational organizations. *Educational Management Administration & Leadership*, *44*(4), 578–598. https://doi.org/10.1177/1741143214558573

Eid, M. (2009). *Sustainable Development & Project Management*. Lambert Academic Publishing, Cologne.

Fischer, B. D., & Charef, L. (2021). Leadership in an agile project management environment. *Journal of Leadership, Accountability and Ethics*, *18*(4). https://doi.org/10.33423/jlae.v18i4.4606

Gartner (2006), "*Achieving agility: defining agility in an IT context*", available at: www.gartner.com/en/documents/491393/achieving-agility-defining-agility-in-an-it-context

Greenleaf, R. K. (2002). *Servant Leadership: A Journey into the Nature of Legitimate Power and Greatness*. Paulist Press, New York.

Gronn, P. (2002). Distributed leadership as a unit of analysis. *The Leadership Quarterly*, *13*(4), 423–451. https://doi.org/10.1016/S1048-9843(02)00120-0

Grzesik, K., & Piwowar-Sulej, K. (2018). Project managers' competencies and leadership styles from the perspective of organizations functioning in Poland. *Journal of Entrepreneurship, Management and Innovation, 14*(3), 35–60. https://doi.org/10.7341/20181432

Hallinger, P., & Suriyankietkaew, S. (2018). Science mapping of the knowledge base on sustainable leadership, 1990–2018. *Sustainability, 10*(12), 4846. https://doi.org/10.3390/su10124846

Harris, A. (2011). Distributed leadership: Implications for the role of the principal. *Journal of Management Development*, *31*(1), 7–17. https://doi.org/10.1108/02621711211190961

Iannotta, M., Meret, C., & Marchetti, G. (2020). Defining leadership in smart contexts: A concept synthesis. *Frontiers in Psychology*, *11*. https://doi.org/10.3389/fpsyg.2020.556933

International Project Management Association (IPMA). (2015). *Individual Competence Baseline for Project, Programme & Portfolio Management. Version 4.0*. IPMA, Zurich.

International Project Management Association (IPMA). (2018). *IPMA Reference Guide ICB4 in an Agile World Version 1.0*. IPMA, Zurich.

Iqbal, Q., & Piwowar-Sulej, K. (2022). Sustainable leadership in higher education institutions: social innovation as a mechanism. *International Journal of Sustainability in Higher Education*, *23*(8), 1–20. https://doi.org/10.1108/IJSHE-04-2021-0162

Jeronen, E. (2013). Sustainability and Sustainable Development. In Idowu, S.O., Capaldi, N., Zu, L., & Gupta, A.D. (Eds), *Encyclopedia of Corporate Social Responsibility* (pp. 2370–2378). Springer, Berlin, Heidelberg. https://doi.org/10.1007/978-3-642-28036-8_662

Lee, H. W. (2017). Sustainable leadership: An empirical investigation of its effect on organizational effectiveness. *International Journal of Organization Theory and Behavior*, *20*(4), 419–453. https://doi.org/10.1108/IJOTB-20-04-2017-B001

Malik, S. J., Ahmed, W. S., Awan, T. M., Farooq, N., & Khalid, M. (2023). Linking Agile Methodology and Transformational Leadership to Project Success through interplay of Team Building. In T. Chakraborty, T. M. Awan, A. Natarajan, & M. Kamran (Eds.), *Agile Leadership for Industry 4.0. An Indispensable Approach for the Digital Era* (pp. 340–362). Apple Academic Press, New York.

Marcelino-Sádaba, S., González-Jaen, L. F., & Pérez-Ezcurdia, A. (2015). Using project management as a way to sustainability. From a comprehensive review to a framework definition. *Journal of Cleaner Production, 99*, 1–16. https://doi.org/10.1016/j.jclepro.2015.03.020

Marnewick, C., Silvius, G., & Schipper, R. (2019). Exploring patterns of sustainability stimuli of project managers. *Sustainability, 11*(18), 5016. https://doi.org/10.3390/su11185016

McCann, J. T., & Holt, R. A. (2010). Defining sustainable leadership. *International Journal of Sustainable Strategic Management, 2*(2), 204–210. https://doi.org/10.1504/IJSSM.2010.032561

McPherson, B. (2016). Agile, adaptive leaders. *Human Resource Management International Digest, 24*(2), 1–3. https://doi.org/10.1108/HRMID-11-2015-0171

Moradi, S., Kähkönen, K., & Aaltonen, K. (2020). Comparison of research and industry views on project managers' competencies. *International Journal of Managing Projects in Business, 13*(3), 543–572. https://doi.org/10.1108/IJMPB-04-2019-0085

Mubarak, N., Khan, J., Safdar, S., Muhammad, S., & Riaz, A. (2022). Ethical leadership in project-based organizations of Pakistan: The role of psychological empowerment and Islamic work ethics. *Management Research Review, 45*(3), 281–299. https://doi.org/10.1108/MRR-08-2020-0536

Muff, K., Liechti, A., & Dyllick, T. (2020). How to apply responsible leadership theory in practice: A competency tool to collaborate on the sustainable development goals. *Corporate Social Responsibility and Environmental Management, 27*(5), 2254–2274. https://doi.org/10.1002/csr.1962

Müller, R., & Turner, J.R. (2007). Matching the project manager's leadership style to project type. *International Journal of Project Management, 25*(1), 21–32. http://dx.doi.org/10.1016/j.ijproman.2006.04.003

Nauman, S., Musawir, A. U., Malik, S. Z., & Munir, H. (2022). Servant leadership and project success: unleashing the missing links of work engagement, project work withdrawal, and project identification. *Project Management Journal, 53*(3), 257–276. https://doi.org/10.1177/87569728221087161

Pearce, C. L., Conger, J. A., & Locke, E. A. (2008). Shared leadership theory. *The leadership quarterly, 19*(5), 622–628. https://doi.org/10.1016/j.leaqua.2008.07.005

Piwowar-Sulej, K. (2021). Organizational culture and project management methodology: Research in the financial industry. *International Journal of Managing Projects in Business, 14*(6), 1270–1289. https://doi.org/10.1108/IJMPB-08-2020-0252

Piwowar-Sulej, K., & Iqbal, Q. (2022). Leadership styles and sustainable performance: A systematic literature review. *Journal of Cleaner Production*, 134600. https://doi.org/10.1016/j.jclepro.2022.134600

Poon, C., & Silvius, G. (2019). Factors that stimulate project managers to consider sustainability; exploring the stimulus patterns of Canadian project managers. *Journal of Management and Sustainability, 9*(2), 90–114. https://doi.org/10.5539/jms.v9n2p90

Prentice, W. C. H. (2004). Understanding leadership. *Harvard Business Review, January*. https://hbr.org/2004/01/understanding-leadership

Project Management Institute (PMI). (2017a). *Project Manager Competency Development (PMCD) Framework Third Edition*. Newtown Square, PA.

Project Management Institute (PMI). (2017b). *A Guide to the Project Management Body of Knowledge (PMBOK® Guide) — Sixth Edition*. Newtown Square, PA.

Project Management Institute (PMI). (2017c). PMI, *Agile Practice Guide, Project Management Institute and Agile Alliance*. Newtown Square, PA.

Rao, M. S. (2013). Smart leadership blends hard and soft skills. *Human Resource Management International Digest, 21*(4), 38–40. https://doi.org/10.1108/HRMID-04-2013-0023

Sabini, L., & Alderman, N. (2021). The paradoxical profession: Project management and the contradictory nature of sustainable project objectives. *Project Management Journal, 52*(4), 379–393. https://doi.org/10.1177/87569728211007660

Silvius, A. G., & Schipper, R. P. (2014). Sustainability in project management competencies: Analyzing the competence gap of project managers. *Journal of Human Resource and Sustainability Studies, 2*, 40–58. http://dx.doi.org/10.4236/jhrss.2014.22005

Silvius, A. J. G., Schipper, R., Planko, J., van den Brink, J., & Köhler, A. (2012). *Sustainability in Project Management*. Gower Publishing, Bovenkarspel.

Silvius, G., & Schipper, R. (2020). Exploring variety in factors that stimulate project managers to address sustainability issues. *International Journal of Project Management, 38*(6), 353–367. https://doi.org/10.1016/j.ijproman.2020.08.003

Špundak, M. (2014). Mixed agile/traditional project management methodology — Reality or illusion? *Procedia – Social and Behavioral Sciences, 119*, 939–948. https://doi.org/10.1016/j.sbspro.2014.03.105

Srivastava, A., Bartol, K. M., & Locke, E. A. (2006). Empowering leadership in management teams: Effects on knowledge sharing, efficacy, and performance. *Academy of Management Journal, 49*(6), 1239–1251. https://doi.org/10.5465/amj.2006.23478718

Turner, R., & Müller, R. (2005). The project manager's leadership style as a success factor on projects: A literature review. *Project Management Journal, 36*(2), 49–61. https://doi.org/10.1177/875697280503600206

Vecchio, R. P., Justin, J. E., & Pearce, C. L. (2010). Empowering leadership: An examination of mediating mechanisms within a hierarchical structure. *The Leadership Quarterly, 21*(3), 530–542. https://doi.org/10.1016/j.leaqua.2010.03.014

Wiek, A., Withycombe, L., & Redman, C. L. (2011). Key competencies in sustainability: A reference framework for academic program development. *Sustainability Science, 6*, 203–218. https://doi.org/10.1007/s11625-011-0132-6

Woods, P. A. (2004). Democratic leadership: Drawing distinctions with distributed leadership. *International journal of leadership in education, 7*(1), 3–26. https://doi.org/10.1080/1360312032000154522

Zhu, J., Liao, Z., Yam, K. C., & Johnson, R. E. (2018). Shared leadership: A state-of-the-art review and future research agenda. *Journal of Organizational Behavior, 39*(7), 834–852. https://doi.org/10.1002/job.2296

7 Team members' competencies in sustainable project management

Małgorzata Tyrańska, Sylwia Wiśniewska, and Robert Szydło

The characteristics and principles of forming a project team[1]

Generally, a team is a group working or doing something in a particular field. On the other hand, the project management team is a group of people with interdisciplinary skills assigned to a project to fulfill specific tasks (Katzenbach & Smith, 2004; Wachowiak & Gregorczyk, 2018). Members of the project team are distinguished by competencies that are complementary to each other, which allows them to play team roles more fully, as well as to work more efficiently and achieve synergy through cooperation and knowledge sharing. It should be noted that the level of differentiation of competencies of project team members depends on the project's implementation. The composition of the interdisciplinary team can be flexible and may change during the project.

Employees of permanent organizational units become members of the team. Their secondment to the team is for the duration of the project based on dual subordination to both the head of the parent organizational unit and the head of the project team. This arrangement corresponds to typical matrix structures. The characteristics of the project team that distinguish it from traditional employee teams include (Lichtarski, 2012):

- Concentration on a specific goal, which is the execution of a well-defined project or the solution of a specific problem,
- temporariness, meaning the dissolution of the team after the completion of an assigned task or the solution of a set problem,
- moving away from authority based on formal authority to expert authority,
- lack of strict division of labor within the team and low level of formalization of activities.

The implementation of projects largely depends on the ability to work as a team; the interaction relations, in this case, are more complex than in repetitive activities and include interaction within the project team, with employees of the permanent structure of the company, and with external partners: the principal suppliers, subcontractors (Trocki et al., 2003).

DOI: 10.4324/9781003356059-8

While creating a project team, it is worth considering several principles (Puszcz et al., 2016; Szymańska, 2012). The first principle refers to the purpose of the project. It should be emphasized that the project team is set up to carry out a specific, unitary task, and once it is completed, it is dissolved. Thus, the project manager, when appointing members to the team, should formulate and present the objective.

The second principle concerns the size of the project team and implies that it should depend on the scale of the project being implemented. In smaller-scale projects, everyone involved can be a permanent team working together. On the other hand, implementing large projects requires the close cooperation of key people who can form a permanent team and the participation of additional members who perform their tasks at a particular time. In this case, the project team structure is impermanent, and project team members should be selected and released according to the project's current needs. Then the role of the project manager is to determine the composition of the central team. This decision by the project manager should be influenced by such factors as the competence needed to carry out the most critical work, the desire to involve people important to the project by including them in the planning and decision-making process, and their availability.

Another principle indicates that the basis of project team members should be expertise. Knowledge is seen as a unique resource of the project team. This statement is based on the following premises: it is attached to the people who possess it; it cannot be easily transferred; the more it is used, the more it gains in value; and the more unused, it disappears (Wachowiak et al., 2004). In knowledge sharing, isolated information or skills are transformed into knowledge resources to serve the project team. Knowledge sharing can include knowledge replication, i.e., the transfer of the same information to a broader group of employees; these resources must be disseminated immediately and permanently to provide users with permanent access; sharing experiences from previously executed projects and documenting them; exchanging current experiences, which leads to the creation of new knowledge. Factors that hinder the process of knowledge sharing are psychological barriers mainly related to the personality and motivation of team members and the perceptive abilities of the recipient, as well as the competitiveness and individualism of employees who often perceive their knowledge as a source of advantage over others (Winkler & Chmielecki, 2015).

In addition to specialized knowledge, the basis of project team members is complementary competencies, ensuring that the same problem is approached from different points of view. Such complementarity and interdisciplinary competence of project team members ensure the effective and efficient implementation of project tasks.

The next principle states that the practical work of the project team depends on the proper selection of members. Selection of the team should be carried out so that colleagues fill the appropriate roles. An imbalance of these roles, or the absence of one, can significantly limit the productivity of a project team.

From the point of view of achieving the project goal, it is also essential to ensure close internal cooperation between project team members. Interaction in teamwork leads to individual team members modifying their behavior in such a way as to gain the approval of the others, such as through good communication or the ability to adapt to the assigned role.

When creating a project team, it is also worth striving for high team compactness, i.e., the degree to which members are connected, feel motivated to stay on the team, and have a sense of shared identity and solidarity. Team compactness also determines the strength of the team's influence on individual members and signifies the degree of its attractiveness. The greater the attractiveness of a team to its members, the more likely members will align their views, goals, and norms of behavior and conduct, such as punctuality, reliability, and responsibility.

The essence of competencies

The confluence of many scientific disciplines, such as pedagogy and andragogy, praxeology, psychology, sociology, and management, shaped the concept of competency. Therefore, many definitions of competencies have been developed over the years.

Pedagogy deals with competencies in terms of education, but understanding the concept itself is not uniform (Paśko, 2016). Okoń (2001) treats competencies as the ability for personal self-realization. This ability is the basic condition for upbringing (Dylak, 1995). Another approach, also from the field of science and pedagogy, defines *competencies* as the result of the learning process, i.e., the ability to display behaviors adequate to the situation, awareness of the needs and effects of behaviors, and taking responsibility for one's actions (Czerepniak-Walczak, 1995).

In praxeology, competencies are understood as the characteristics of an entity that allow it to perform work effectively. It is a competence that determines the efficiency of action (Stańczyk, 2002).

In psychology, approaches to competence include four aspects (Tucholska, 2005). These are the motivational tendency and needs, the belief in self-efficacy, the determinant of functioning, and the complex dimension of personality determinants of effectiveness and actions. White (1963) defines the motivational aspect of human activity as the basis for exploring the world. Deci and Ryan (2000) developed a self-direction theory based on White's theory. Competence as self-efficacy refers to the subjective perception of the necessity of having a given competency in coping with a problem (Smith, 1974; Bandura, 1989; Cherniss, 1993). The concept of competence as a determinant of good functioning is associated with concepts such as well-being, maturity, mental health, or optimal adjustment. Heath (1977) shows that only mature people can adapt effectively to complex environmental conditions. The last aspect of understanding competencies refers less to a person than to an individual that is closely related to the social environment. Referring to praxeological concepts, competencies are understood as a set of features that allow for effective interaction with an individual's social environment (McClelland, 1973; Raven, 1977).

In management science, ambiguity is not only the result of translation or language translations but also of the common, colloquial understanding of this term. Thus, in the literature on the subject, one can come across competencies as the scope of duties, the individual characteristics of a person, and the level of performance of activities.

Simply understanding the concept is not enough. It is necessary to refer both to the sources of scientific cognition and the first contemporary understandings of competence so that a uniform understanding of the term can be obtained later, thanks to the analysis of definitions.

According to Kotter (1982), how employee competencies are currently defined has been shaped by three research trends: structuralism, phenomenology, and behaviorism. Structuralism focuses on explaining meaning not on the basis of inherited characteristics, but on the basis of the relationship between the elements of the system (Naughton et al., 2010), because that is where the nature of the phenomenon lies. This approach makes it possible to discover deeper relationships than those visible to the naked eye (Levi-Strauss, 1972). Structuralism uses many methods and tools (Lounsbury & Ventresca, 2003). The phenomenological approach is based on the fact that it is not important to delve into the essence of connections and dependencies, and phenomena that are analyzed, i.e., specific, observable phenomena (Bayne & Montague, 2011). Thus, competencies from a phenomenological perspective are related to the perception of given elements and the thought processes and experiences of the individual. Behaviorism is the third research trend shaping the concept of employee competencies. It focuses on stimuli and the behaviors caused by them (Graham, 2019) manifested in various forms. The most significant representatives of behaviorism were Iwan Pawlow and John Watson (classical conditioning), Edward Thorndike (operant conditioning), and Burthus Skinner (operating conditioning). In the context of competence, the following aspects of behaviorism are important: emphasizing individual behavior while ignoring attitudes, focusing on skills from this perspective; competencies are subject to modification through stimuli related to procedures, e.g., organizational culture or stimuli related to contacts in the work environment, for example, the intervention of a superior.

Klieme, Hartig, and Rauch (2008) point to three concepts of competence, focusing on the cognitive approach, the normative concept of education, and the pragmatic approach.

The psychology of the 1970s presented an interesting pragmatic approach to competence. McClelland (1973) postulated a departure from intelligence tests in favor of testing competencies as the ability to cope with specific situations. Diagnosing in terms of competencies was aimed at orienting the process of diagnosing competencies to more real-life situations. The focus was on the effectiveness of the action, not the cognitive or educational aspect.

According to Tyrańska (2015), competencies mean a person's essential attributes, personality traits, education, professional experience, knowledge, skills and abilities, and practical aspects of their use in performing tasks at the workplace. Pocztowski (2018) defines *competencies* as a cluster of permanent properties/characteristics of an individual, constituting a configuration of knowledge, skills, abilities, motives, and values, enabling high performance and other above-average achievements in a specific area and context of professional activity.

Project team member competencies and sustainable project management

An approach focused solely on increasing cost efficiency and maximizing profit becomes increasingly difficult to sustain. Thus, for the industry to provide true prosperity for all concerned, i.e., investors, employees, and consumers, its goal must include social and environmental issues. Sustainable development is seen as a process of transformation that ensures that the needs of the present generation are met without diminishing the development opportunities of future generations, including through integrated economic, social, and environmental development activities. This understanding of sustainable development was popularized through a 1987 report entitled "Our Common Future", prepared under the direction of Norwegian Environment Minister G. H. Brundtland (known as the Brundtland Report), who headed the United Nations Commission on Environment and Development (Adamczyk, 2018).

Further development of sustainable development was continued in 1992 at the Earth Summit, which resulted in the Agenda 21 document. Another milestone of sustainable development efforts was the United Nations Millennium Declaration, which set out the Millennium Development Goals (MDGs). Their implementation was supposed to make it possible to effectively face the challenges of the 21st century in the run-up to 2015. The provisions of the 1992 summit were renewed in 2002 in Johannesburg and then at the 2012 summit in Rio de Janeiro, referred to as Rio+20 under the declaration The Future We Want. The MDGs were replaced in 2015 by the Sustainable Development Goals, included in the Transforming Our World: The 2030 Agenda for Sustainable Development (Manowska, 2020).

The purpose of sustainable development is to preemptively eliminate, or at least reduce, the imbalance between economic growth and social development and between socioeconomic development and the natural environment (Trzepacz, 2012). The guiding idea of the sustainability concept is being extended to various areas of business operations, including the project management process. In this sense, it is noted that measuring the success of a project only from the classic mechanistic perspective, namely, scope, time, and budget, is insufficient, and this opens space for a new approach to measuring the success of a project, considered from three points: social, economic, and environmental at each stage of the project life cycle (Yang & Yang, 2015; Ansah & Sorooshian, 2017; Hamdan, 2021).

Nowadays, the project management process integrates with the sustainability approach. The value of a project is created based on its social, economic, and environmental results, which are delivered to the various stakeholders involved. Generating value from implemented projects is synonymous with equality, prosperity, social growth, respect for shared resources, working for the quality of life, and preserving humanity (Tam, 2010; Silvius & Schipper, 2014; Moldovan et al., 2022).

De Haan (2006) introduced a model of "Gestaltungskompetenz" developed into the set of critical competencies for sustainable development. Those are competencies for:

Table 7.1 Sustainable competencies in project management competencies model ICB-3

Sustainability competencies	*ICB3 Project management competencies*		
	Technical competencies	*Behavioral competencies*	*Contextual competencies*
Systems thinking competencies	-	-	Partial coverage (specifically 3.05 Permanent organization, 3.06 Business, 3.07 Systems, products & technology)
Anticipatory competencies	-	-	-
Normative competencies	-	Limited coverage (specifically 2.15 Ethics, 2.14 Values appreciation)	-
Strategic competencies	"Full" coverage	-	Partial coverage (specifically 3.09 Health, security, safety & environment)
Interpersonal competencies	-	"Full" coverage	-

Source: Silvious and Schipper (2014).

1. perspective-taking,
2. anticipation,
3. interdisciplinary knowledge acquisition,
4. dealing with incomplete and overly complicated information,
5. cooperation,
6. dealing with individual decision-making dilemmas,
7. participation,
8. motivation,
9. reflecting of goals,
10. moral action,
11. independent action,
12. supporting others.

The abovementioned competencies are reflected in ICB-3 (IPMA, 2006), which is a model for project management competencies: (behavioral, technical, and contextual) and are presented in Table 7.1.

De Rezende and Blackwell (2019) introduced a project manager competencies framework that comprises 81 competencies divided across 11 dimensions

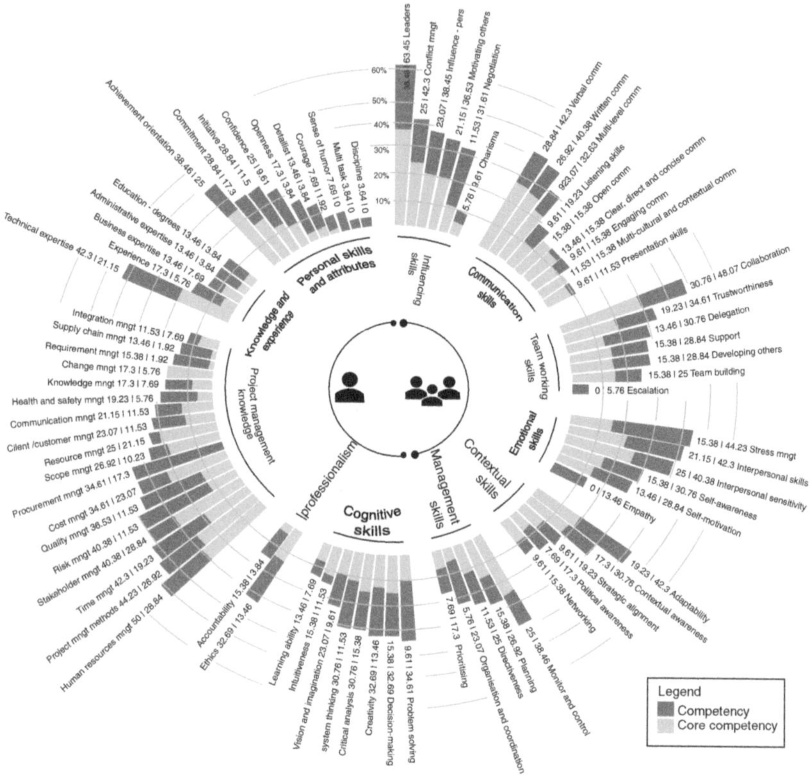

Figure 7.1 Framework for project management competencies.

Source: De Rezende and Blackwell (2019).

(Figure 7.1) such as: influencing, communication, teamwork, emotional, contextual, management, cognitive skills, professionalism, knowledge and experience, project management knowledge, and personal skills and attributes.

Several out of 81 competencies are intertwined with the Brundiers et al. (2020) concept of sustainable competencies framework. Those are system thinking, strategic thinking, interpersonal skills, and problem-solving.

As a result of the synthesis of the literature (Figure 7.2), Stanitas, Kirytopoulos, and Leopoulos (2021) introduced the model of the top eight values of project management that might provide a sustainable approach. It is essential to state that the values can also be considered competencies.

All three abovementioned concepts provide a deep understanding of the most critical competencies in creating and maintaining sustainable project management. It is then crucial to state that competencies that appear in at least two models are:

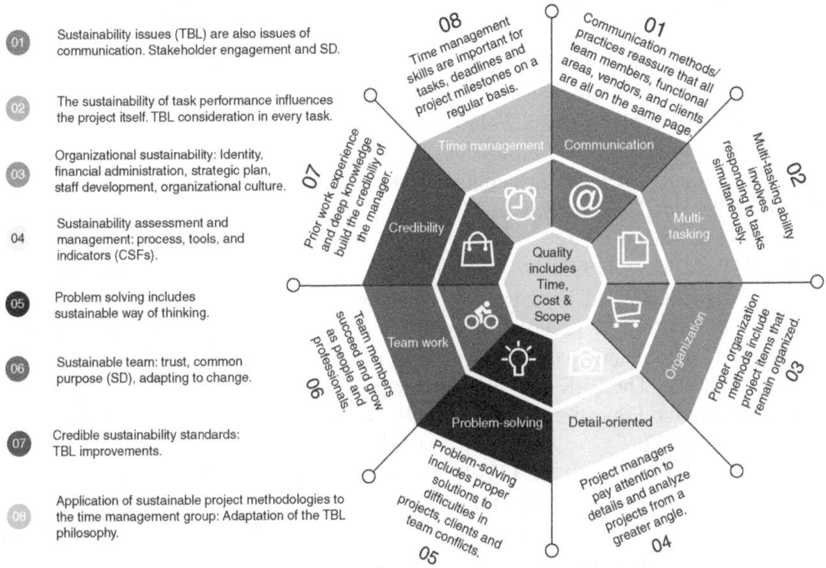

Figure 7.2 Sustainable project management practices and supporting competencies.

Source: Stanitas, Kirytopoulos, and Leopoulos (2021).

1 interpersonal competence,
2 strategic thinking,
3 organization,
4 business and project management competence,
5 system thinking,
6 problem-solving.

Note

1 The publication was financed from the subsidy granted to the Cracow University of Economics – Project nr 067/ZZS/2022/POT.

References

Adamczyk, J. (2018). Zrównoważony rozwój jako paradygmat współczesnego zarządzania przedsiębiorstwem. *Przegląd Organizacji, 12*, 8–14.

Ansah, R. H., & Sorooshian, S. (2017). Effect of lean tools to control external environment risks of construction projects. *Sustainable Cities and Society, 32*, 348–356. https://doi.org/10.1016/j.scs.2017.03.02

Bandura, A. (1989). Human agency in social cognitive theory. *American Psychologist, 44*, 1175–1184.

Bayne, T., & Montague, M. (2011). Cognitive phenomenology: An introduction. In T. Bayne, & M. Montague (Eds.), *Cognitive Phenomenology* (pp. 1–34). Oxford: Oxford University Press.

Brundiers, K., Barth, M., Cebrián, G. et al. (2021). Key competencies in sustainability in higher education—Toward an agreed-upon reference framework. *Sustainability Science, 16*, 13–29. https://doi.org/10.1007/s11625-020-00838-2

Cherniss, C. (1993). Role of professional self-efficacy in the etiology and amelioration of burnout. In W. B. Schaufeli, C. Maslach, & T. Marek (Eds.), *Professional Burnout: Recent Developments in Theory and Research* (pp. 135–149). Washington, DC: Taylor & Francis.

Czerepniak-Walczak, M. (1995). *Między dostosowaniem a zmianą. Elementy emancypacyjnej teorii edukacji.* Katowice: Wydawnictwo Naukowe US.

Deci, E. L., & Ryan, R. M. (2000). The "what" and "why" of goal pursuits: Human needs and the self-determinantion of behavior. *Psychological Inquiry, 11*, 227–268.

de Haan, G. (2006). The BLK "21" Programme in Germany: A "Gestaltungskompetenz"-Based Model for Education for Sustainable Development. *Environmental Education Research, 1*, 19–32.

de Rezende, L.B, Blackwell, P. (2019). Project management competency framework. *Iberoamerican Journal of Project Management, 10*(1), *34–59.*

Dylak, S. (1995). *Wizualizacja w kształceniu nauczycieli.* Poznań: Wydawnictwo Uniwersytetu Adamia Mickiewicza w Poznaniu.

Graham, G. (2019). Behaviorism. In E. N. Zalta (Ed.), *The Stanford Encyclopedia of Philosophy.* Stanford: Stanford University. https://plato.stanford.edu/entries/behaviorism/

Hamdan, H. A. M., Andersen, P. H., & de Boer, L. (2021). Stakeholder collaboration in sustainable neighborhood projects: A review and research agenda. *Sustainable Cities and Society, 68*, 102776. https://doi.org/10.1016/j.scs.2021.102776

Heath, D. H. (1977). *Maturity and Competence. A Transcultural View.* New York: Gardner Press.

IPMA (2006). *IPMA Competence Baseline Version 3.0.* International Project Management Association, Nijkerk.

Katzenbach, J. R., & Smith D. K. (2004). *Siła zespołów: wpływ pracy zespołowej na efektywność organizacji.* Kraków: Oficyna Ekonomiczna.

Klieme, E., Hartig, J., & Rauch, D. P. (2018). The concept of competence in educational contexts. In E. Klieme, J. Hartig, & D. Leutner (Eds.), *Assessment of Competencies in Educational Contexts* (pp. 3–22). Newburyport: Hogrefe & Huber.

Kotter, J. P. (1982). *The General Managers.* London: Collier Macmilan.

Levi-Strauss, C. (1972). *Structuralism and Ecology*. Bernard Alumnae.

Lichtarski, J. M. (2012). Motywowanie członków zespołu zadaniowego w teorii i w praktyce. *Nauki o Zarządzaniu, 1*(10), 58–67.

Lounsbury, M., & Ventresca, M. (2003). The new structuralism in organizational theory. *Organization, 10*(3), 457–480.

Manowska, A. (2020). Koncepcja zrównoważonego rozwoju w procesie podejmowania decyzji związanych z funkcjonowaniem terenów przygranicznych — powiat cieszyński. *Śląsk Cieszyński w świetle wyzwań i zagrożeń XXI wieku "TRANSCARPATHICA"*, VII, 115–135. https://doi.org/10.34916/tc.2020.07.07.

McClelland, D. C. (1973). Testing for competence rather than for "intelligence". *American Psychologist, 28*, 1–14.

Moldovan, F., Blaga, P., Moldovan, L., & Bataga, T. (2022). An innovative framework for sustainable development in healthcare: The human rights assessment. *International Journal of Environmental Research and Public Health, 19*(4), 2222. http://dx.doi.org/10.3390/ijerph19042222

Naughton, G. M., Rolfe, S. A., & Siraj-Blatchford, I. (2010). *Doing Early Childhood Research.* Berkshire: Open University Press.

Okoń, W. (2001). *Nowy słownik pedagogiczny.* Warszawa: Wydawnictwo Akademickie "Żak".

Paśko, N. (2016). Rozważania o kompetencjach pedagogicznych nauczycieli edukacji wczesnoszkolnej. *Pedagogika Przedszkolna i Wczesnoszkolna, 4*(7), 105–119.

Pocztowski, A. (2018). *Zarządzanie zasobami ludzkimi: Koncepcje, praktyki, wyzwania.* Warszawa: Polskie Wydawnictwo Ekonomiczne.

Puszcz, H., Dąbrowski, Ł., & Zaborek, M. (2016). *Zespoły po polsku: jak firmy działające na polskim rynku podnoszą swoją efektywność pracy dzięki pracy zespołowej.* Gliwice: One Press.

Raven, J. (1977). On the components of competence and their development in education. *Teachers College Record, 78*, pp. 457–475.

Silvius, A. J. G., & Schipper, R. P. J. (2014). Sustainability in project management: a literature review and impact analysis. *Social Business, 4*(1), 63–96. https://doi.org/10.1362/204440814X13948909253866

Smith, M. B. (1974). Competence and adaptation. *The American Journal of Occupational Therapy, 28*, pp. 11–15.

Stańczyk, P. (2002). Prakseologiczne spojrzenie na kompetencje. *Prace Naukowe Akademii Ekonomicznej we Wrocławiu. Nauki Humanistyczne* (937), 189–194.

Stanitsas, M., Kirytopoulos, K., Leopoulos, V. (2021). Integrating sustainability indicators into project management: The case of construction industry. *Journal of Cleaner Production, 279*, 123774, ISSN 0959-6526, https://doi.org/10.1016/j.jclepro.2020.123774

Szymańska, K. (2012). Przegląd współczesnych poglądów na zarządzanie zasobami ludzkimi w projektach. *Rocznik Naukowy Wydziału Zarządzania w Ciechanowie, 1-4*, 129–149.

Tam, G. C. K. (2010). The program management process with sustainability considerations. *Journal of Project, Program & Portfolio Management, 1*(1), 17–27. https://doi.org/10.5130/pppm.v1i1.1574

Trocki, M., Grucza, B., & Ogonek, K. (2003). *Zarządzanie projektami.* Warszawa: Polskie Wydawnictwo Ekonomiczne.

Trzepacz, P. (2012). Geneza i istota koncepcji rozwoju zrównoważonego. W. P. Trzepacz (Ed)., *Zrównoważony rozwój – wyzwania globalne: podręcznik dla uczestników studiów doktoranckich* (13–35). Kraków: Instytut Geografii i Gospodarki Przestrzennej UJ.

Tucholska, K. (2005). Zagadnienie kompetencji w psychologii. *Roczniki psychologiczne, 8*(2), pp. 11–36.

Tyrańska, M. (2015). *Koncepcja systemu oceny kompetencji kadry menedżerskiej w przedsiębiorstwie.* Kraków: Wydawnictwo Uniwersytetu Ekonomicznego w Krakowie.

Wachowiak, P., & Gregorczyk, S. (2018). Kompetencje kierowników zespołu projektowego. *Studia i Prace Kolegium Zarządzania i Finansów, 159*, 75–91.

Wachowiak, P., Gregorczyk, S., Grucza, B., & Ogonek, K. (2004). *Kierowanie zespołem projektowym.* Warszawa: Difin.

White, R. W. (1963). Motivation reconsidered: The concept of competence. In E. J. Shoben, & F. L. Ruch (Eds.), *Perspectives in Psychology* (pp. 33–59). Scott: Foresman & Co.

Winkler, R., & Chmielecki M. (2015). Komunikacja a dzielenie się wiedzą w projektowych zespołach międzykulturowych. *Zeszyty Naukowe Uniwersytetu Ekonomicznego w Krakowie, 939*, 87–99. https://doi.org/10.15678/ZNUEK.2015.0939.0306

Yang, J., & Yang, Z. (2015). Critical factors affecting the implementation of sustainable housing in Australia. *Journal of Housing and the Built Environment, 30*, 275–292. https://doi.org/10.1007/s10901-014-9406-5

Index

agile project 15
agile project management 44, 45, 92
agile project manager 115
agility 10, 11, 16, 26, 113

competencies 108, 128
complexity 16, 17, 26

environmental orientation 53

future research 46, 104, 120

green project management 90

Industry 4.0 73
IPMA 90, 109

nonprofit organizations 87

PMBOK 110
PMI 40, 109
polysemy 7
project leadership 114
project management methodologies 14, 91, 92, 108, 114
project manager 108
project stakeholders 37, 56, 82
project success 36, 41, 55, 59, 64
project team 126

scales of projects 25
sustainability 20, 26, 36, 42
sustainability/sustainable competencies 114, 131, 133
sustainable dynamics abilities 51
sustainable project management 1, 22, 88

waterfall 90

For Product Safety Concerns and Information please contact our EU representative GPSR@taylorandfrancis.com Taylor & Francis Verlag GmbH, Kaufingerstraße 24, 80331 München, Germany